Matchbox Puppets

Alan & Brenda Stockwell

VESPER HAWK

ISBN 978-0-9565013-3-2

www.vesperhawk.com

To make a puppet from the book you will need
    A Household Size matchbox
    Photocopies on thin A4 card of the head and body of the chosen puppet
    Colouring materials
    Scissors and glue

All the puppets in this book are made on the same principle.

A matchbox forms the basis of the head. The matchbox is prepared in a special way so that when the drawer or tray of the matchbox is slid open and closed it makes the puppet's mouth open and close as if it were talking.

The most suitable matchbox to use is the large household size. Other similar boxes are called Cook's Matches. The heads and bodies of the puppets in the book are of the correct size for photocopying. If you should use a smaller box eg "Swan Vestas" you will have to set the photocopier to reduce to an appropriate size. Guidance will be found at the end of the book.

The way of preparing your matchbox is set out on the next page.

The head of the puppet is simply coloured with paints or crayons then cut out. The mouth part is indicated on the head by dotted lines. This is cut out separately. The bulk of the head is glued to the front cover of the box, the mouth piece is glued to the tray of the box. This is clearly shown on page 5.

The body of the puppet, as with the head, is simply coloured and cut out. It is attached by glue or sticky-tape to the back of the matchbox sleeve (outer cover).

A few of the simpler puppets at the beginning of the book do not have a body at all. They are just talking heads.

SLEEVE (front view)   TRAY

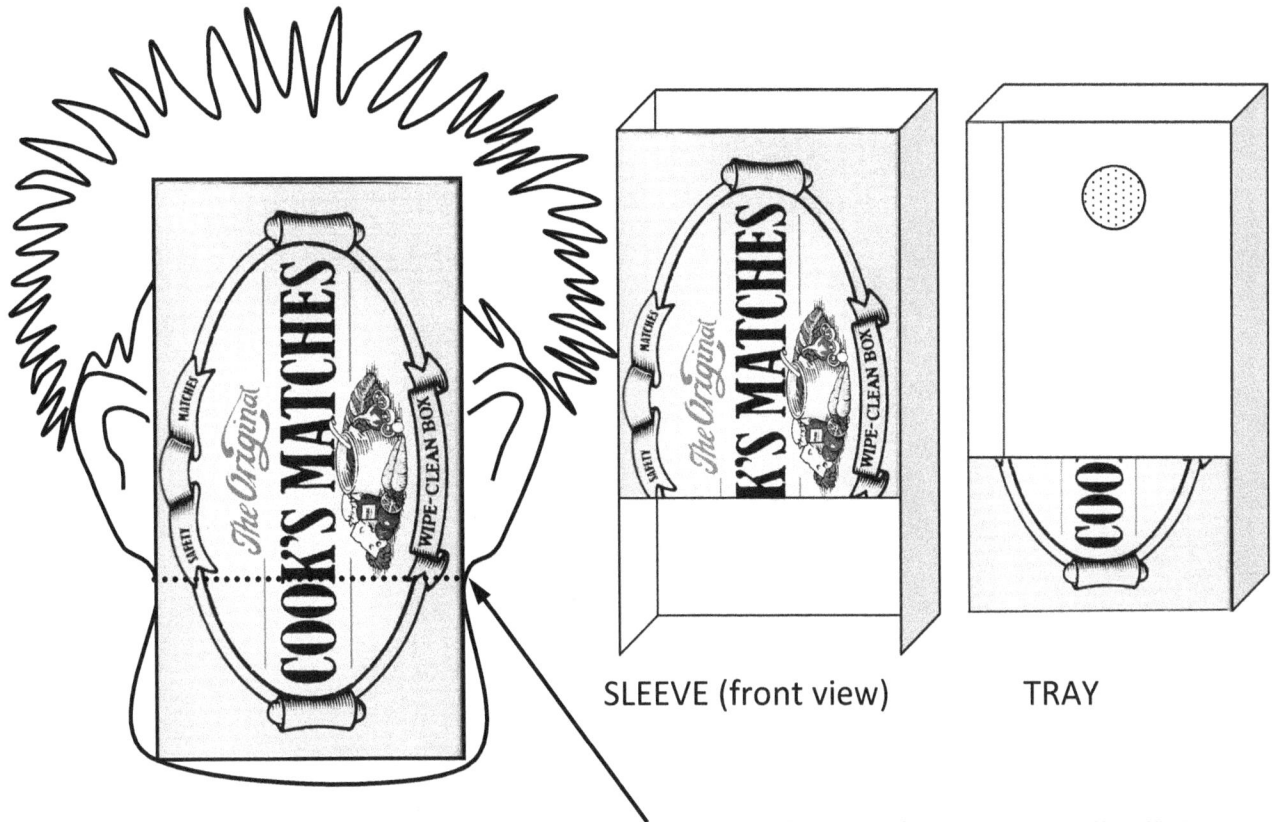

Note whereabouts on the face the dotted line divides the mouth and mark position on front of matchbox sleeve

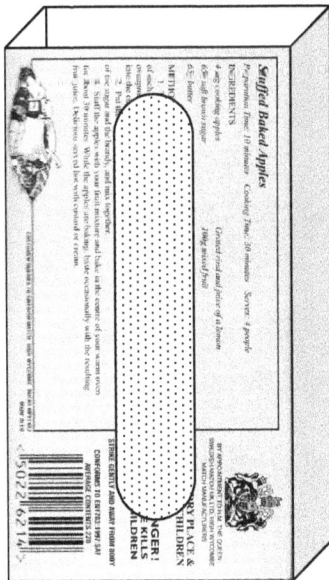

SLEEVE (back view)

- Take a large household size matchbox, empty out the contents and separate into SLEEVE and TRAY

- Lay the SLEEVE on the face so that the bottom of the box lies within the bottom line of the face. Note where the dotted line bisects the mouth and mark it on the box

- Cut along the marked line from the front of the SLEEVE

- Stick the cut-off portion (which will vary from ¼ to a ⅓ in most cases) on to the TRAY. When the TRAY is replaced in the SLEEVE the cut-off portion will appear in its former position

- In the bottom of the TRAY cut a hole at the other end to where you glued the portion of cover

- In the back of the SLEEVE make a long slot

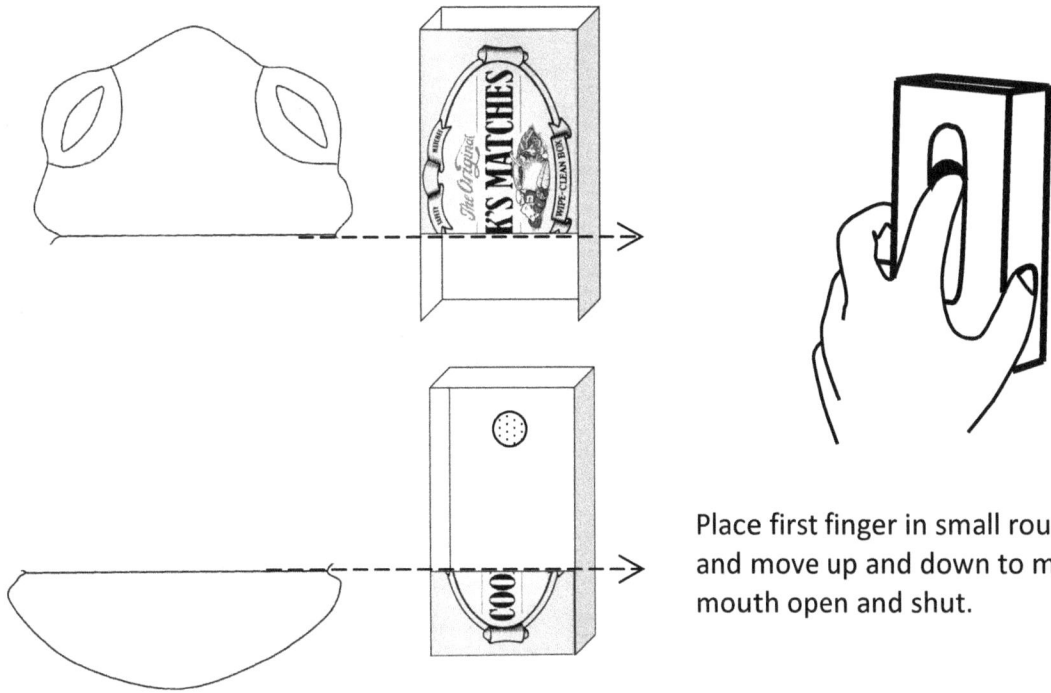

Front view

Place first finger in small round hole and move up and down to make mouth open and shut.

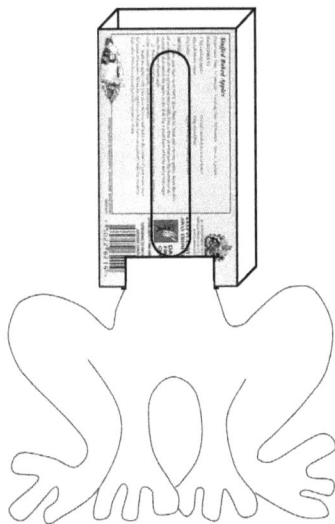

Back view

- Colour your head and cut it out.

- Glue the top part to the sleeve of the matchbox.

- Glue the mouth part to the tray of the matchbox.

- Colour your body and cut it out.

- Glue the body to the back of the matchbox.

And that's it!

Note that on some heads the mouth piece will not occupy the full width of the head. The outlines alongside indicate the position of the box in such cases.

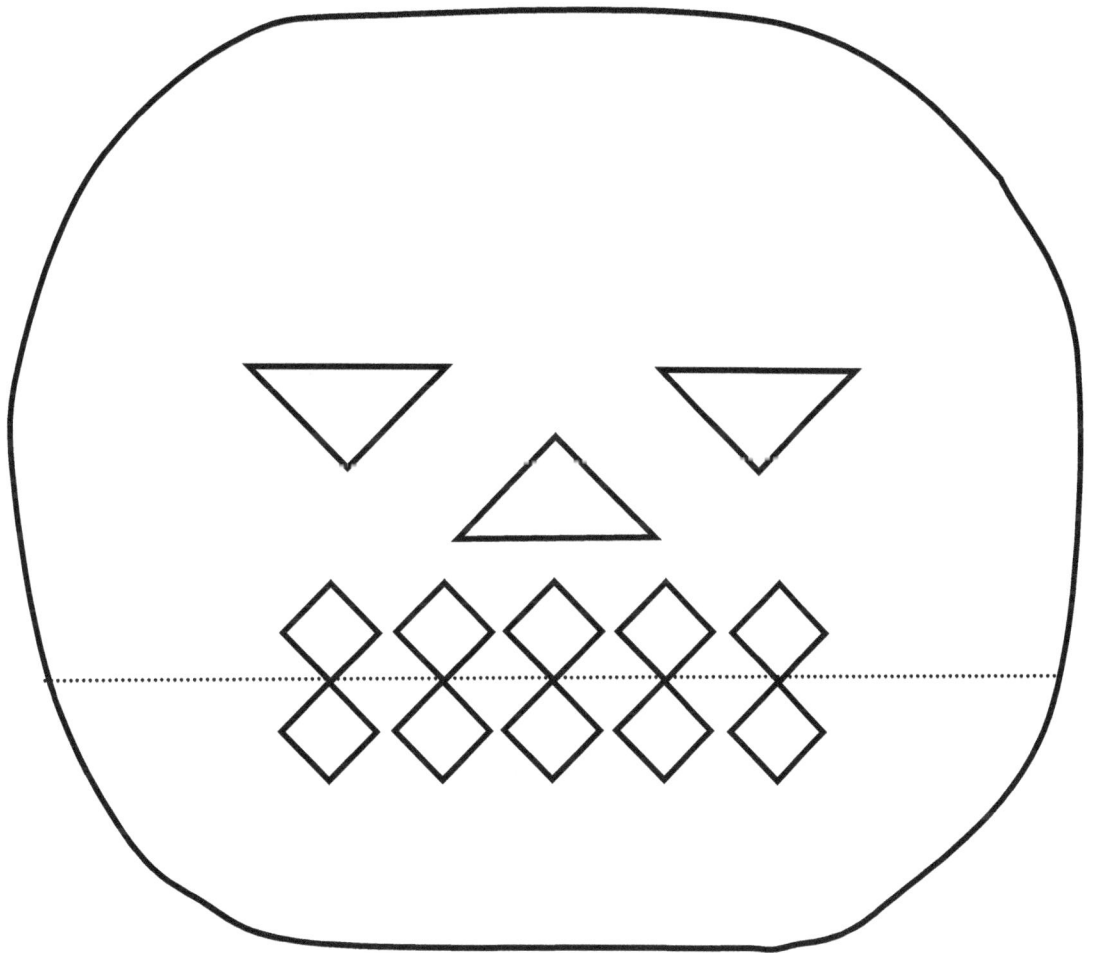

APPLE

Showing position of matchbox

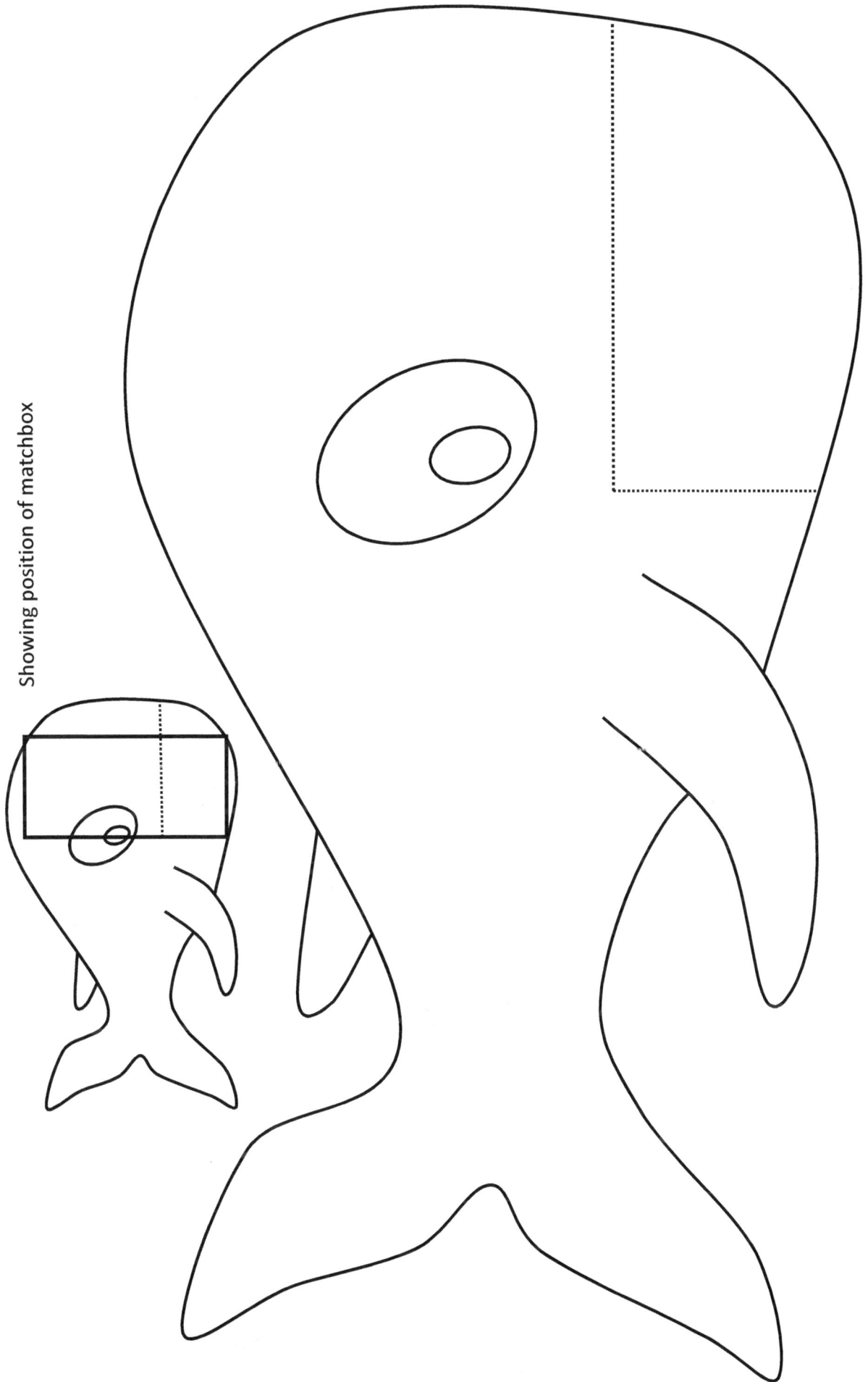

NB: For the mouth of this puppet use a **small** matchbox. The tail is attached by a short length of thread knotted on either side or a small paper fastener. Bend the tail at the dotted line so that you have a grip to wag it.

NB: This puppet uses a **Small** matchbox for the mouth movement

FROG (Head)

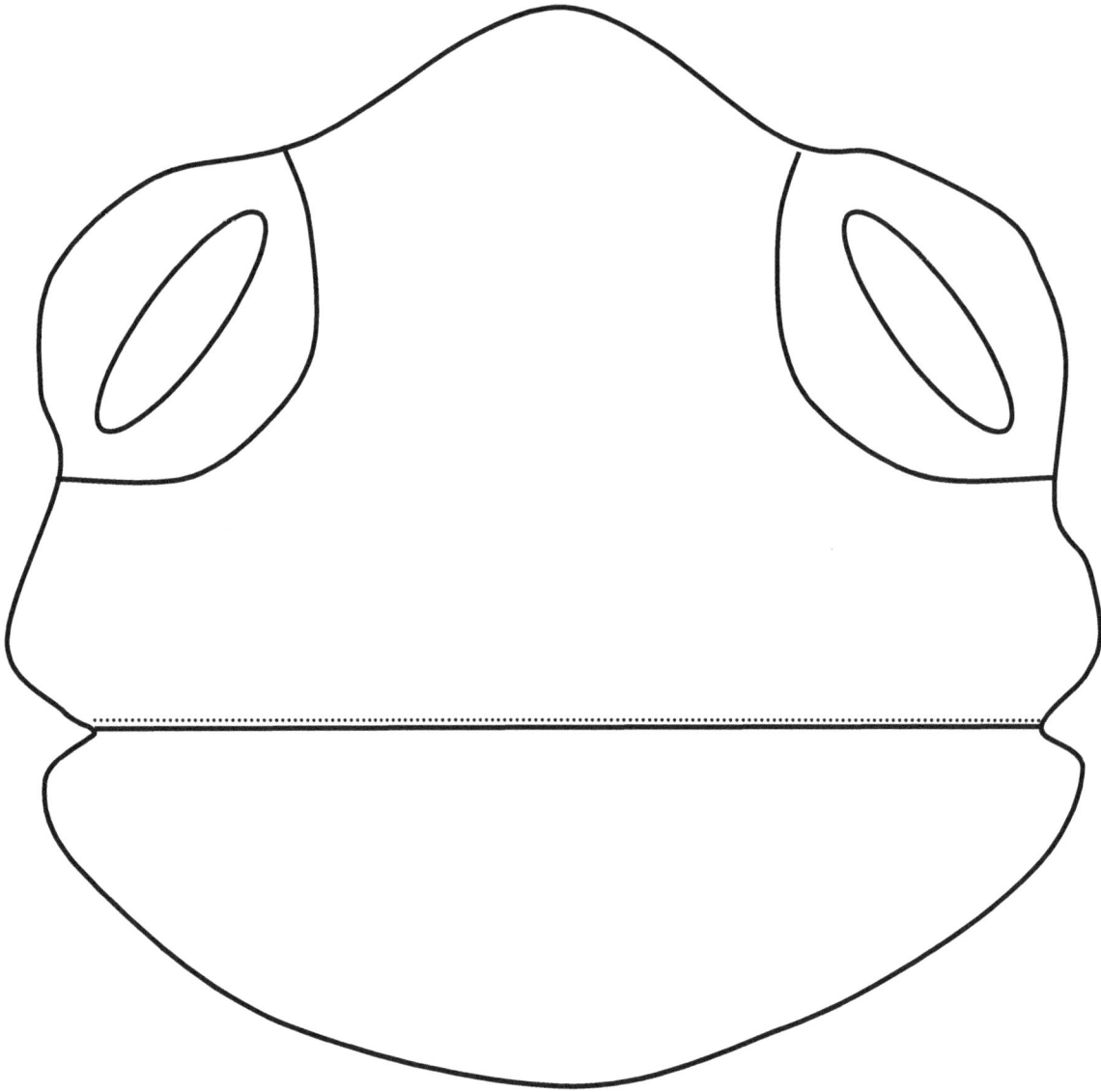

For the FROG puppet you can save colouring by
copying on to green card!

PIG (Head)

For the PIG puppet you can save colouring by
copying on to pink card!

CAT (Head)

RABBIT (Head)

RABBIT (Head)

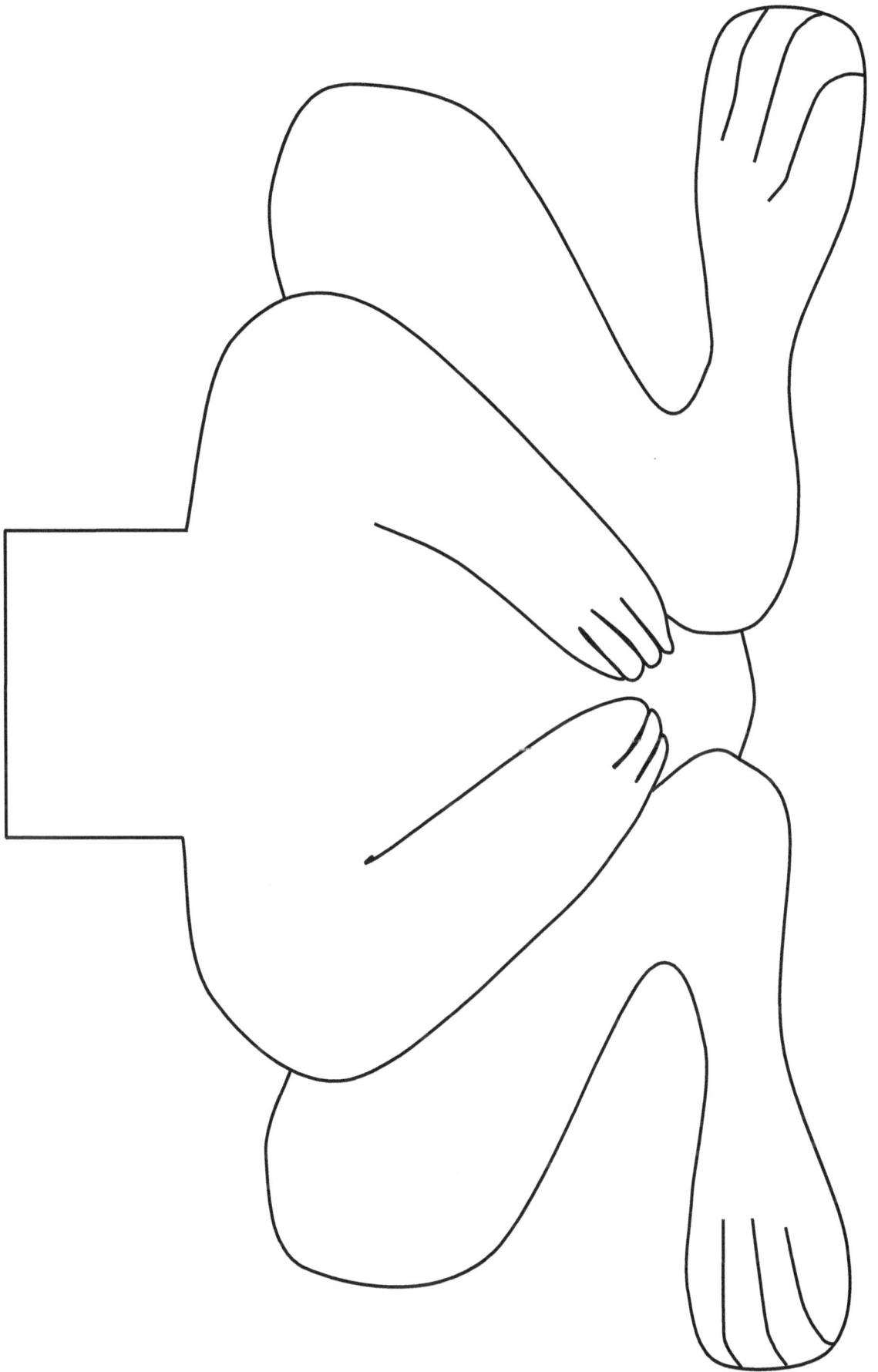

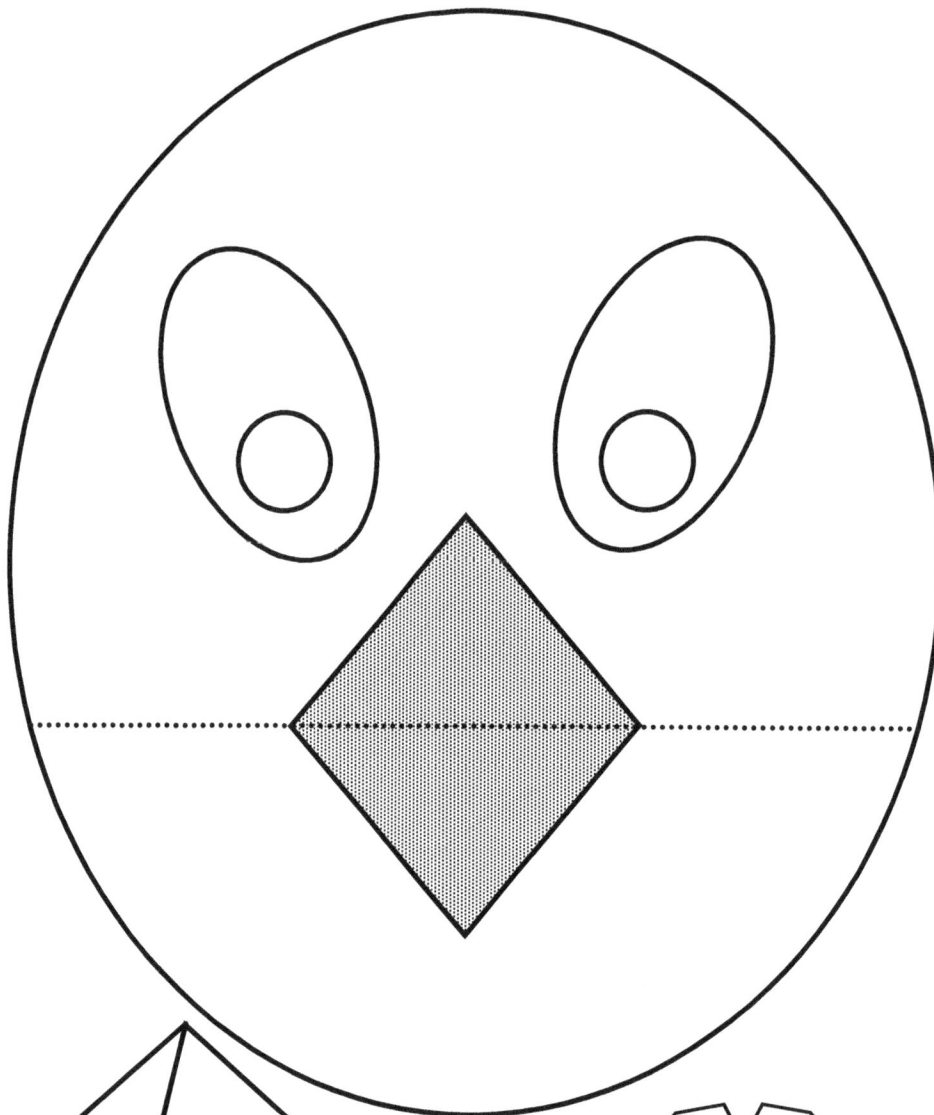

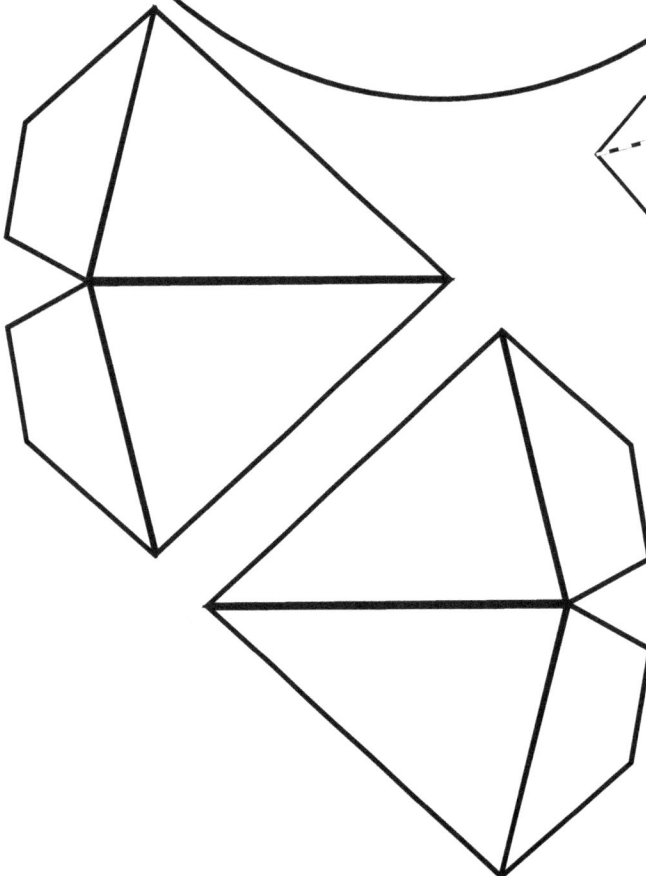

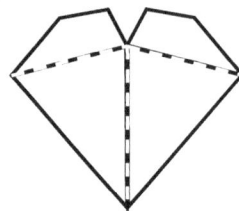

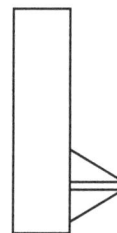

Fold the upper and lower beaks on dashed lines as shown on small diagram above and glue in position on shaded portions.

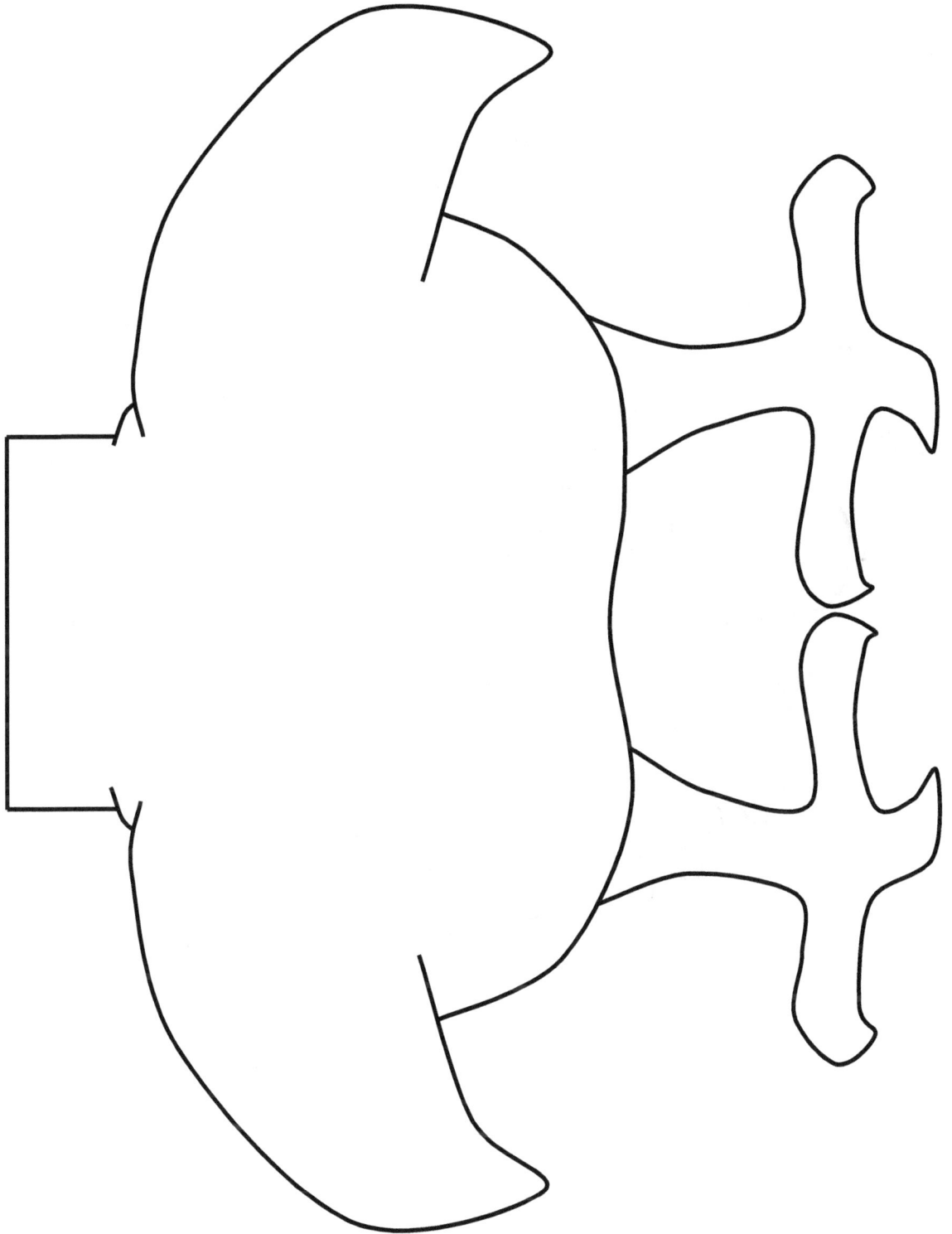

MONKEY (Head)

MONKEY (Head)

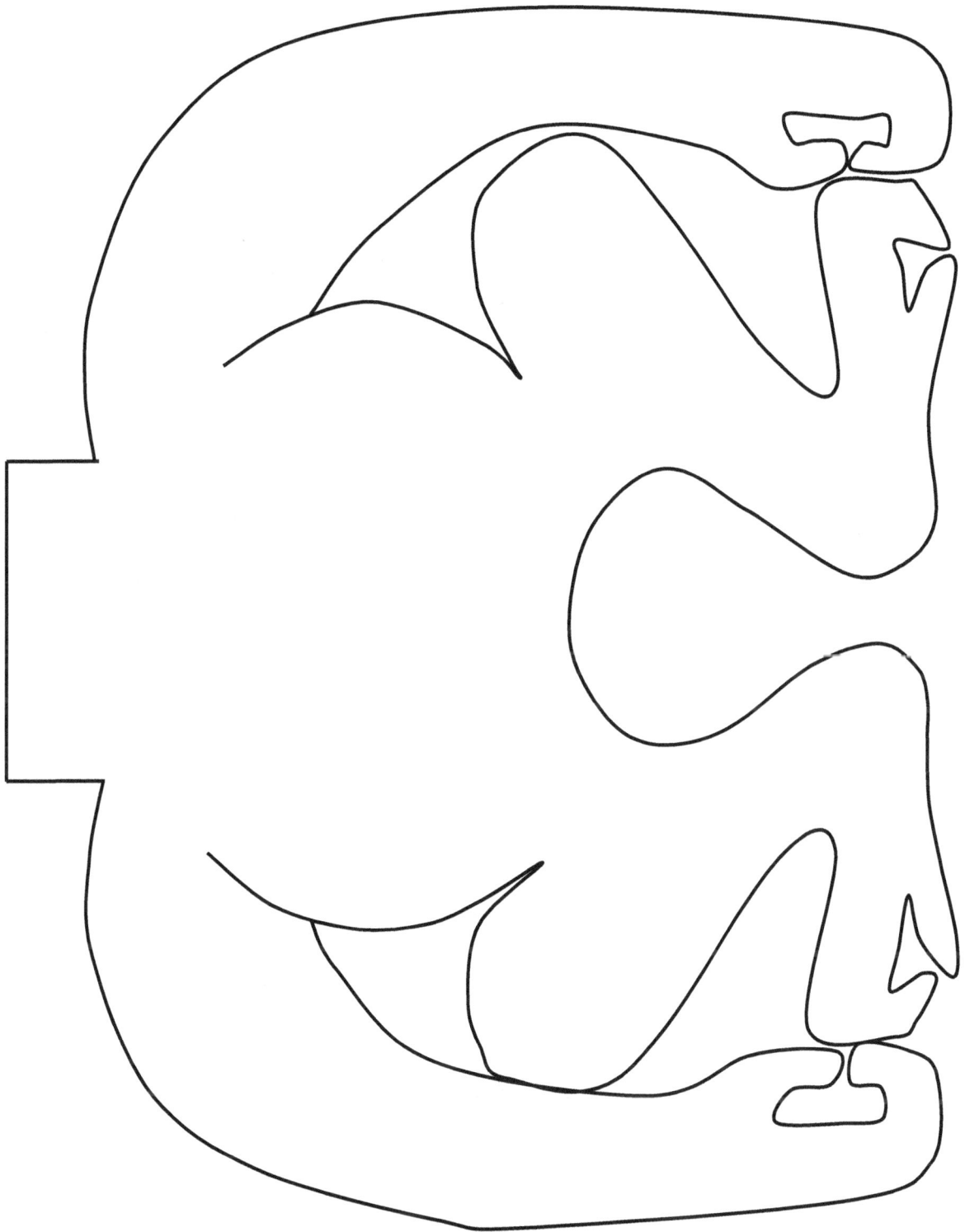

LION (Head)

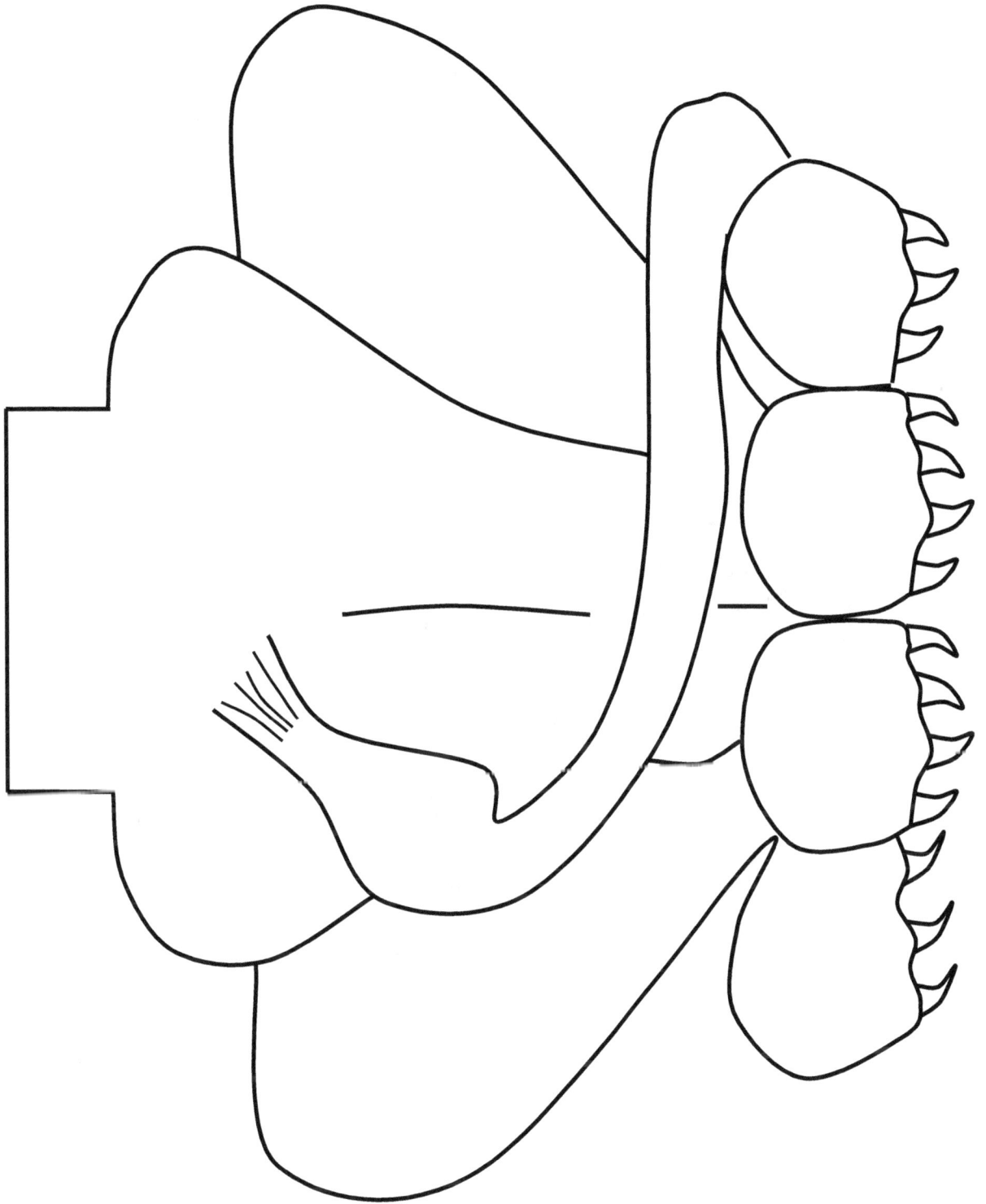

OCTOPUS (Head)

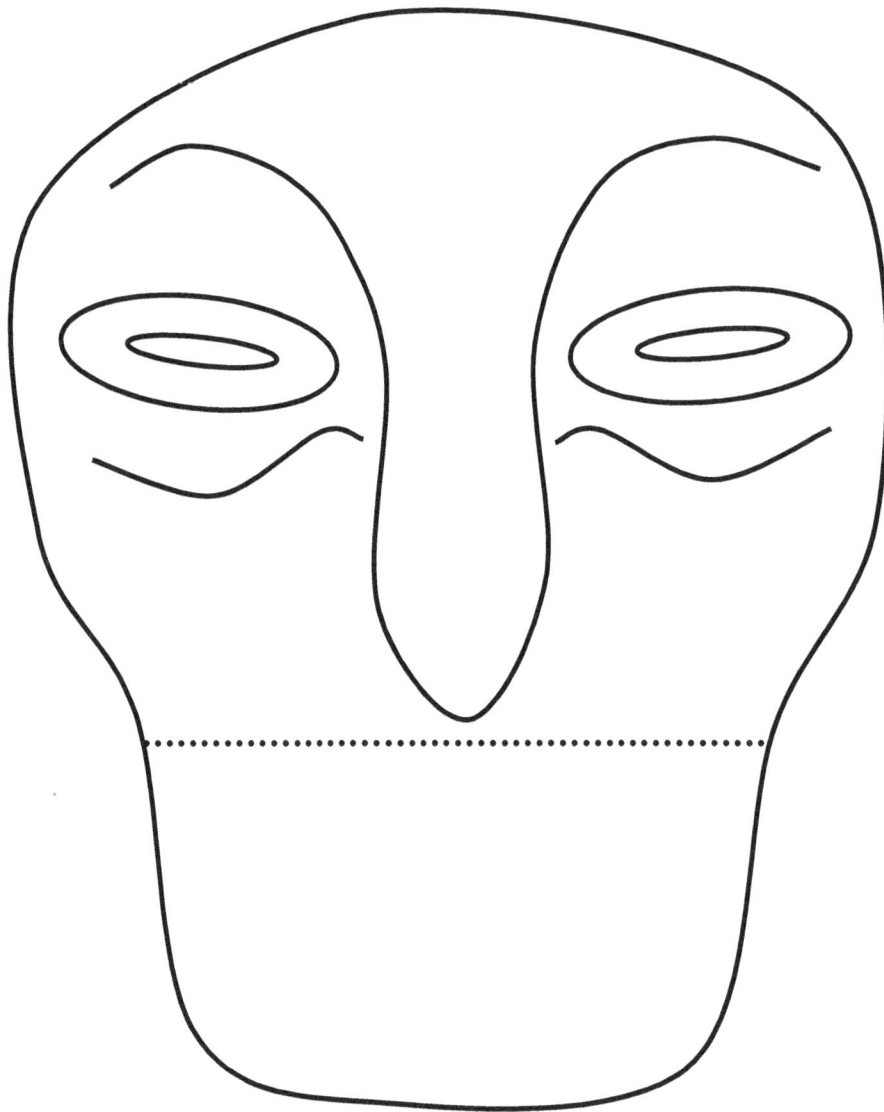

OCTOPUS (Head)

DINOSAUR (Head)

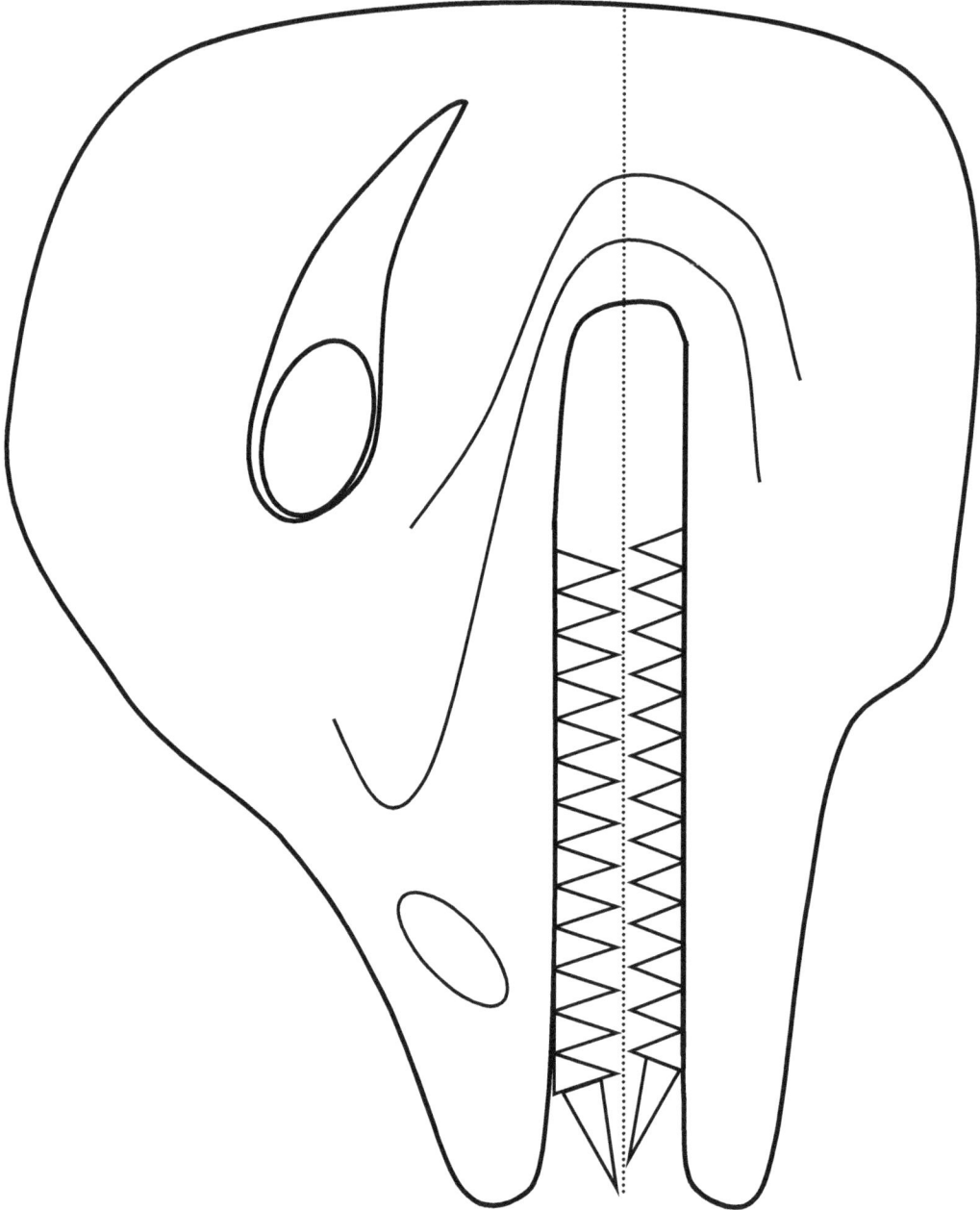

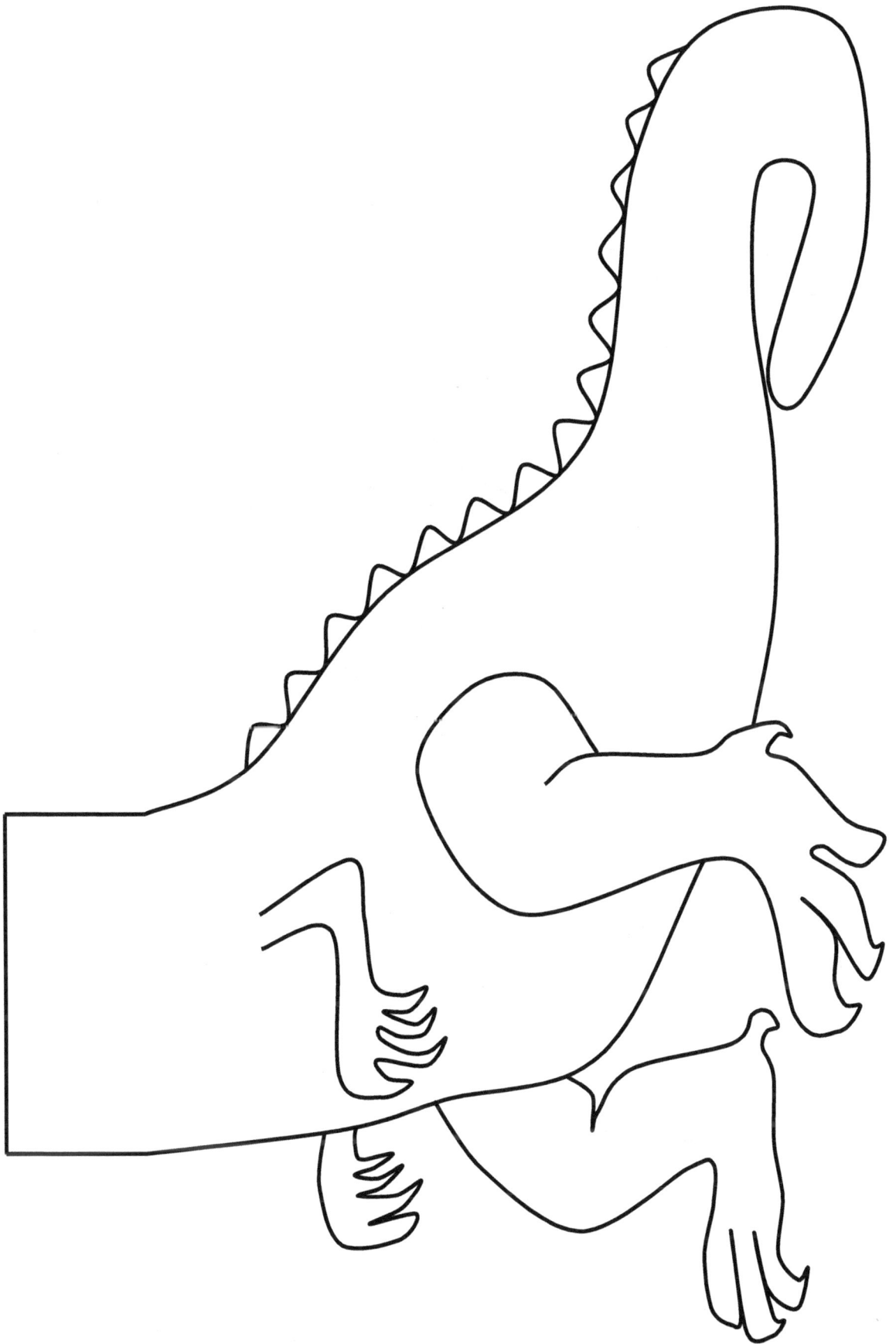

TEDDY BEAR (Head)

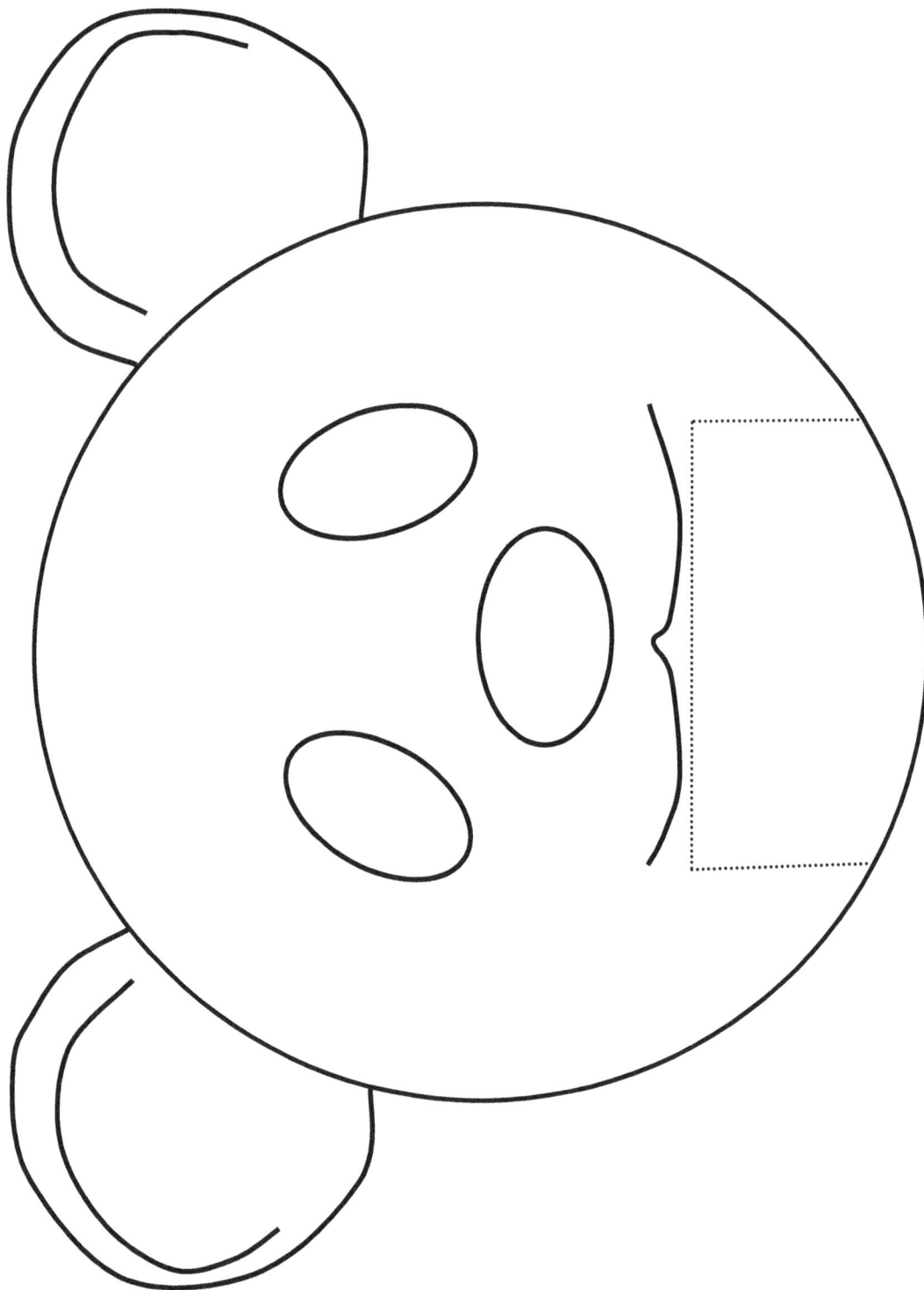

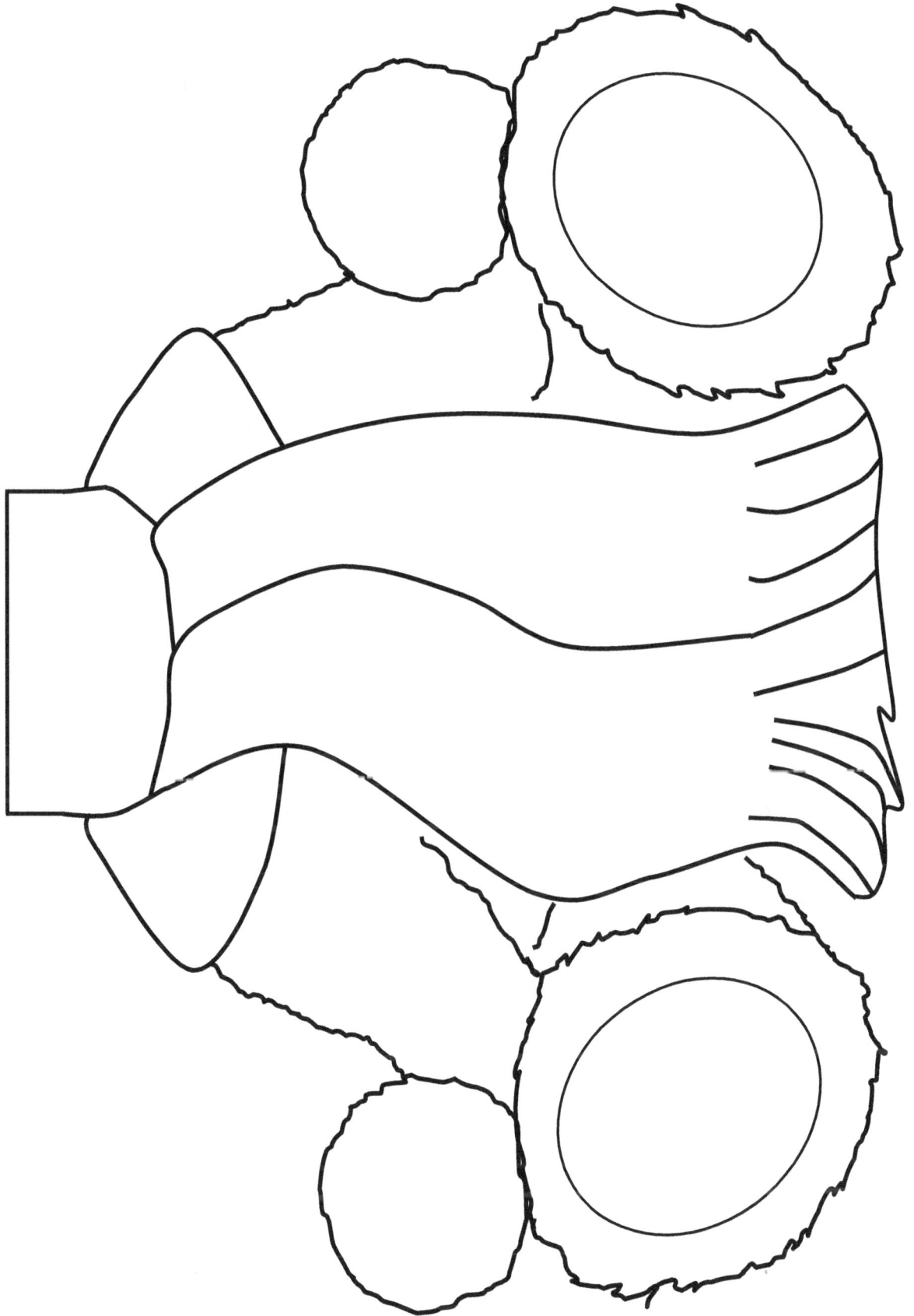

SCARECROW (Head)

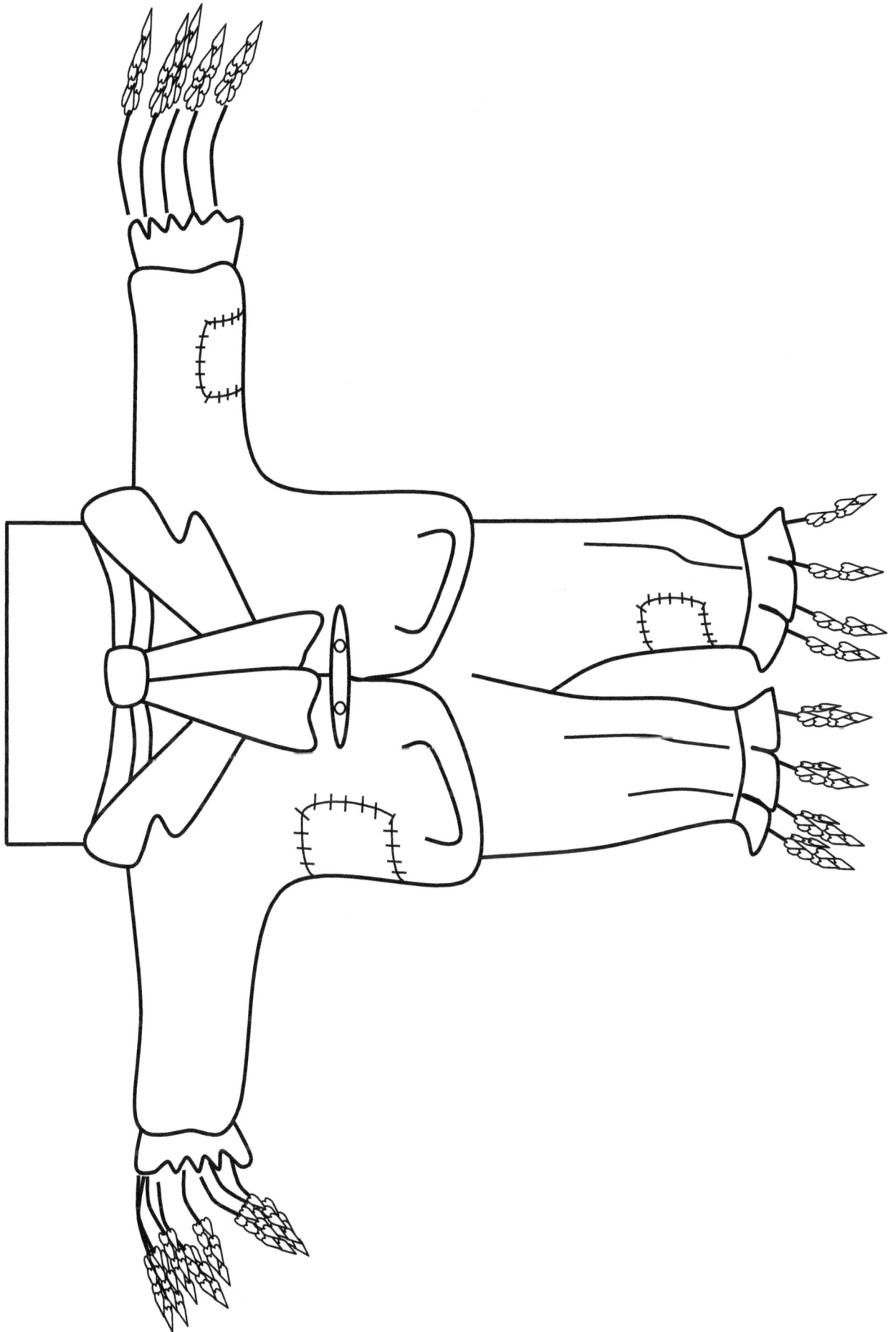

BALLET DANCER (Head)

BALLET DANCER (Head)

COWBOY (Head)

KING (Head)

Attach moustache to top lip

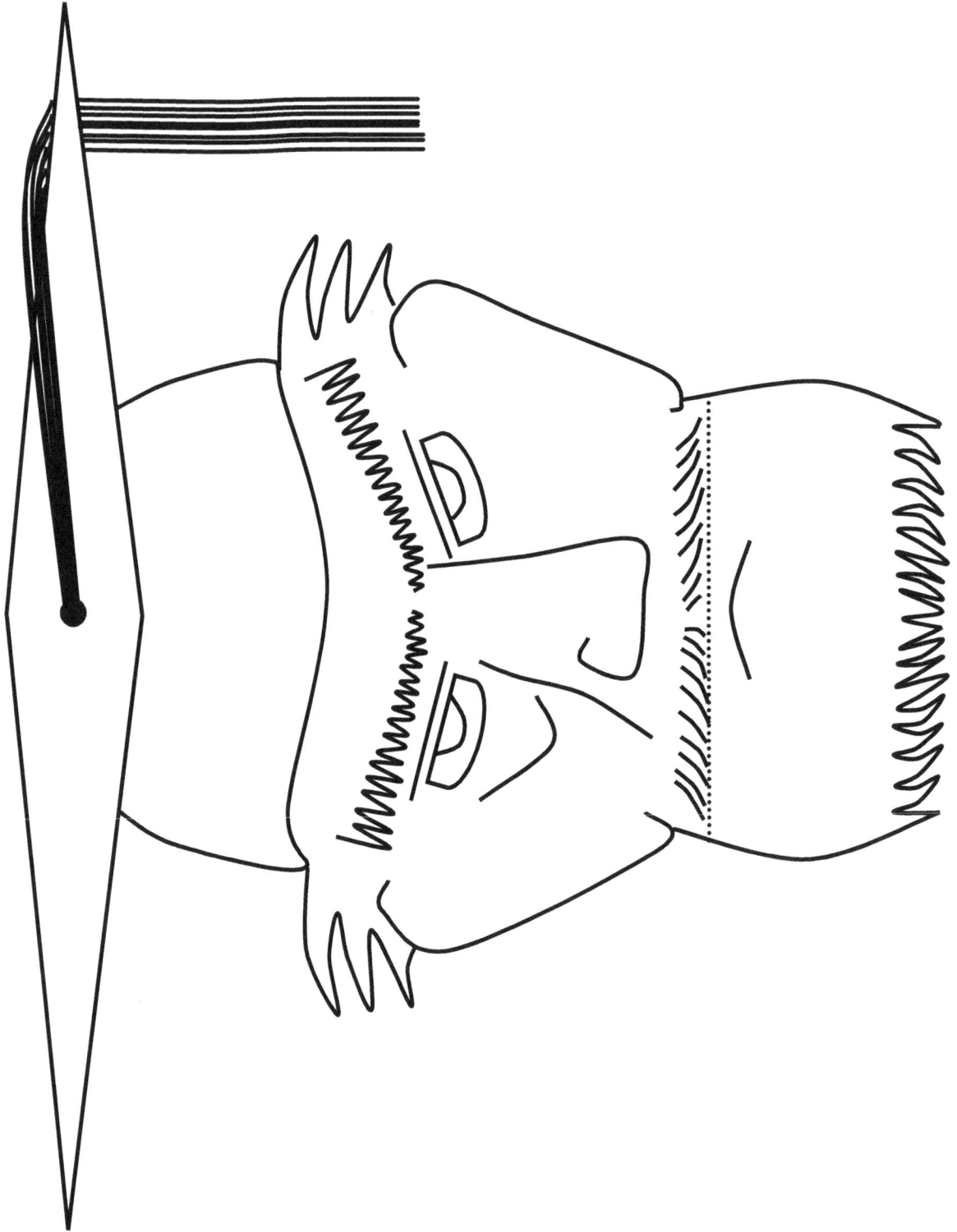

SCHOOLBOY (Head)

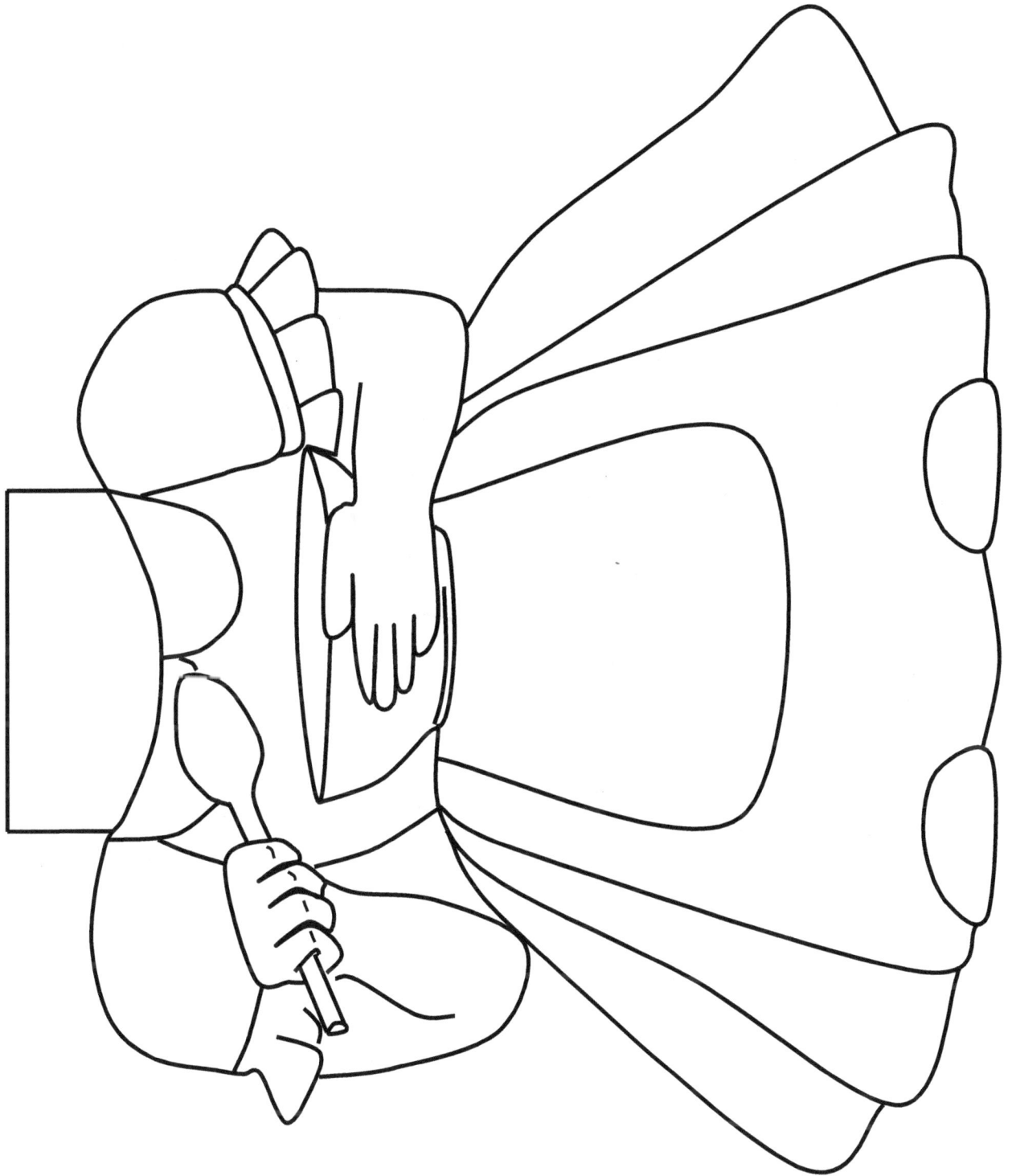

Position of matchbox

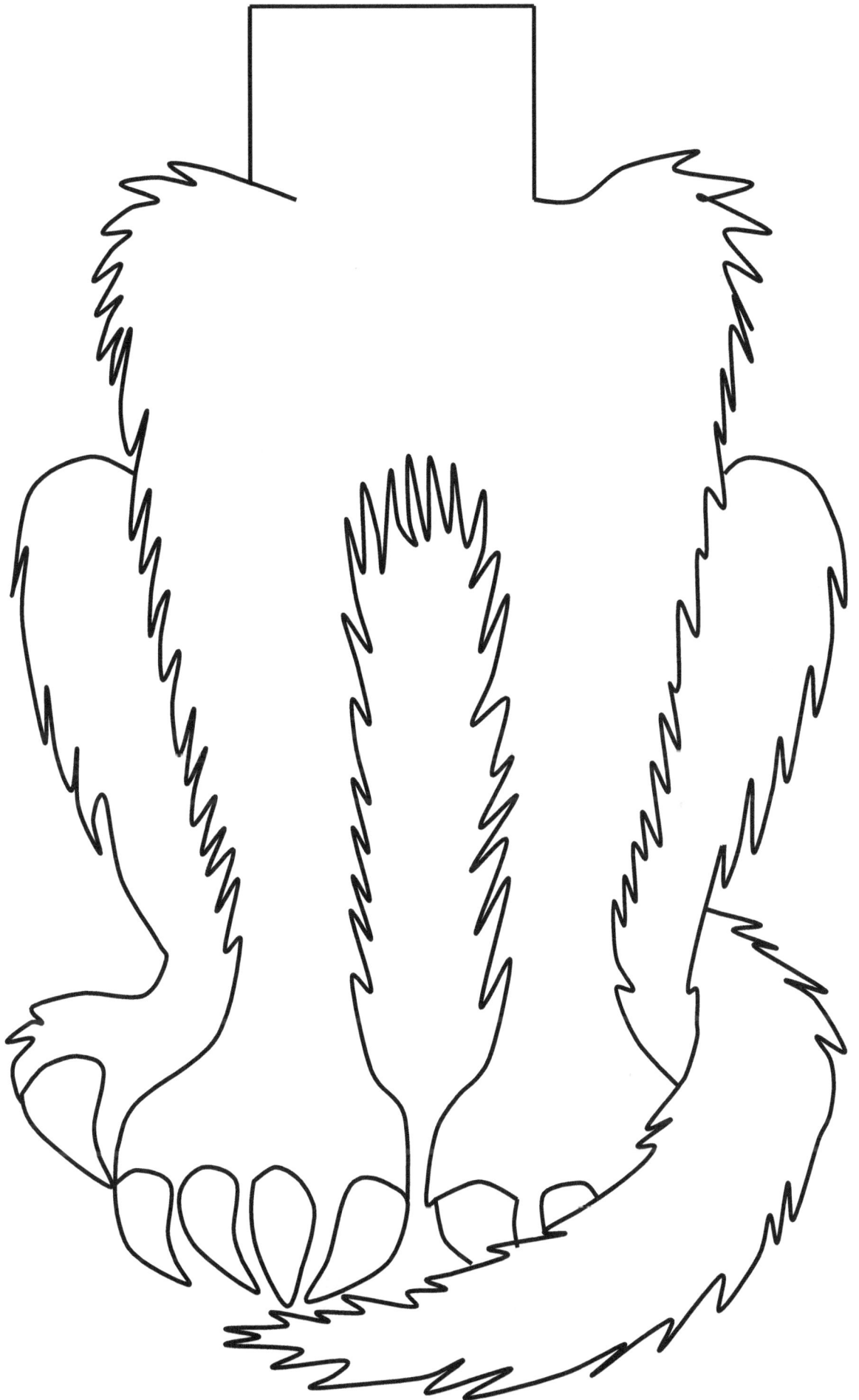

WOLF AS GRANNY (Head) Red Riding Hood Set

Glue jaw piece on moving part of matchbox allowing
the teeth to slide up in front of face above.

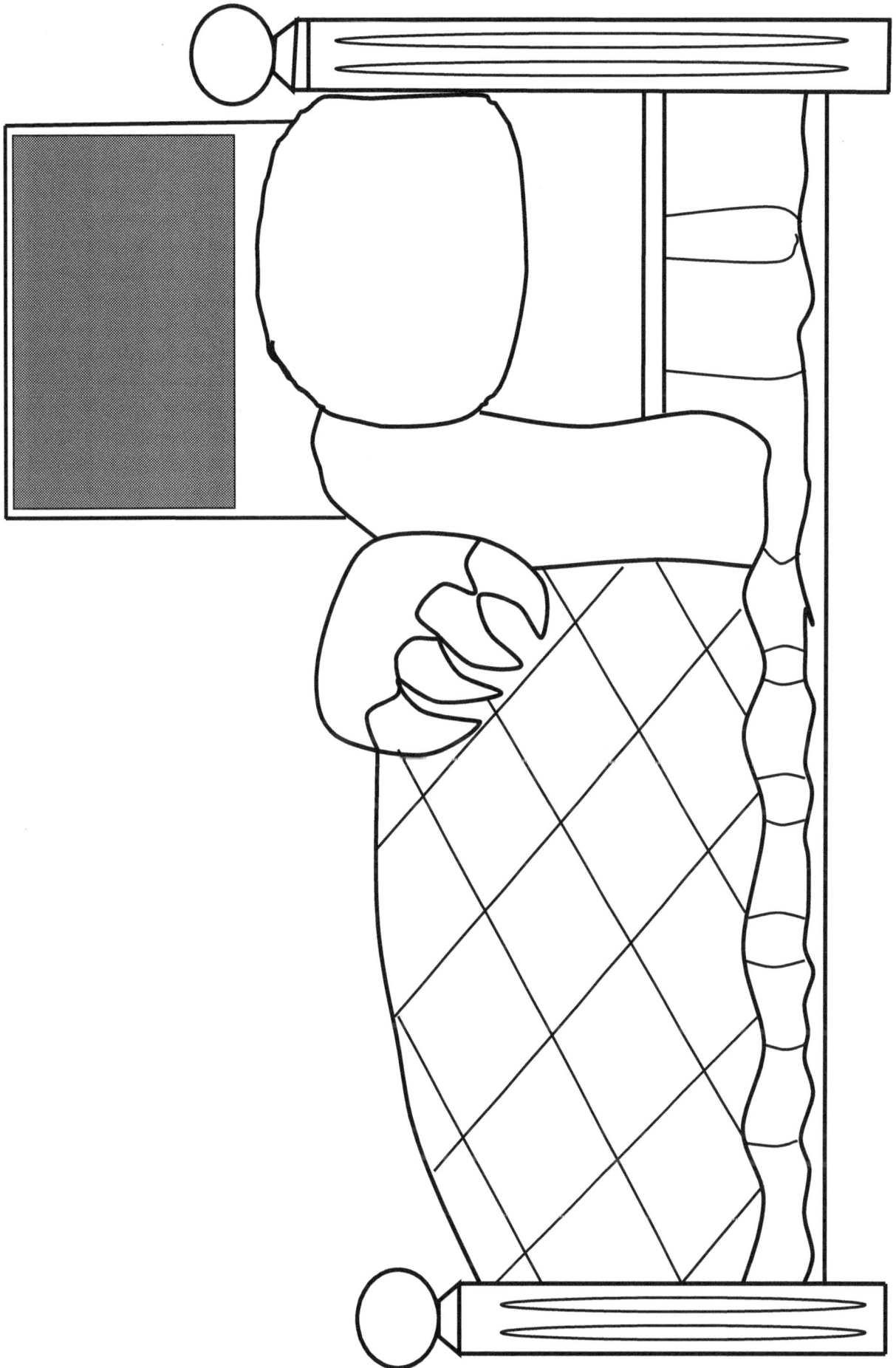

FATHER CHRISTMAS (Head)

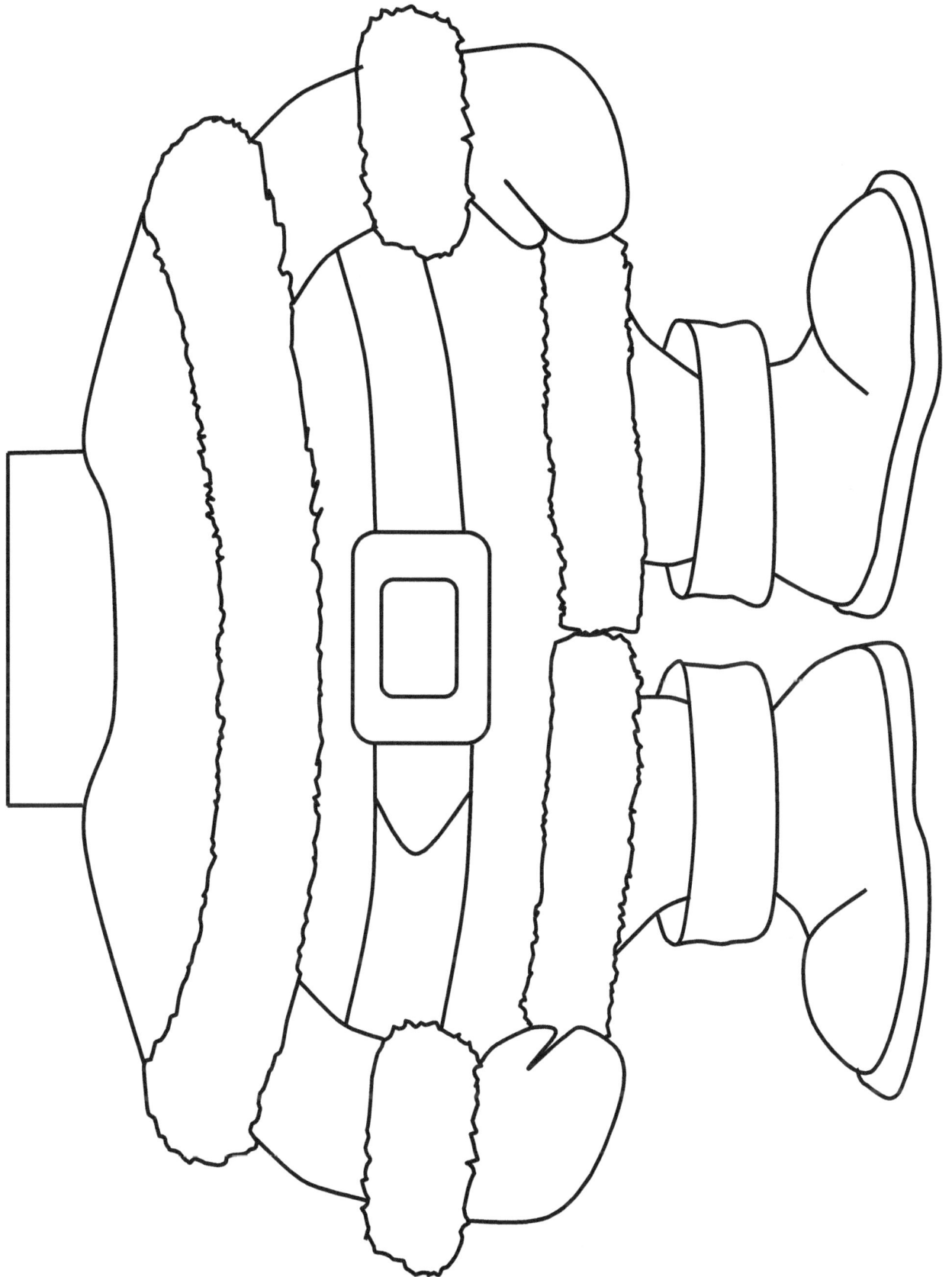

RUDOLF (Head)

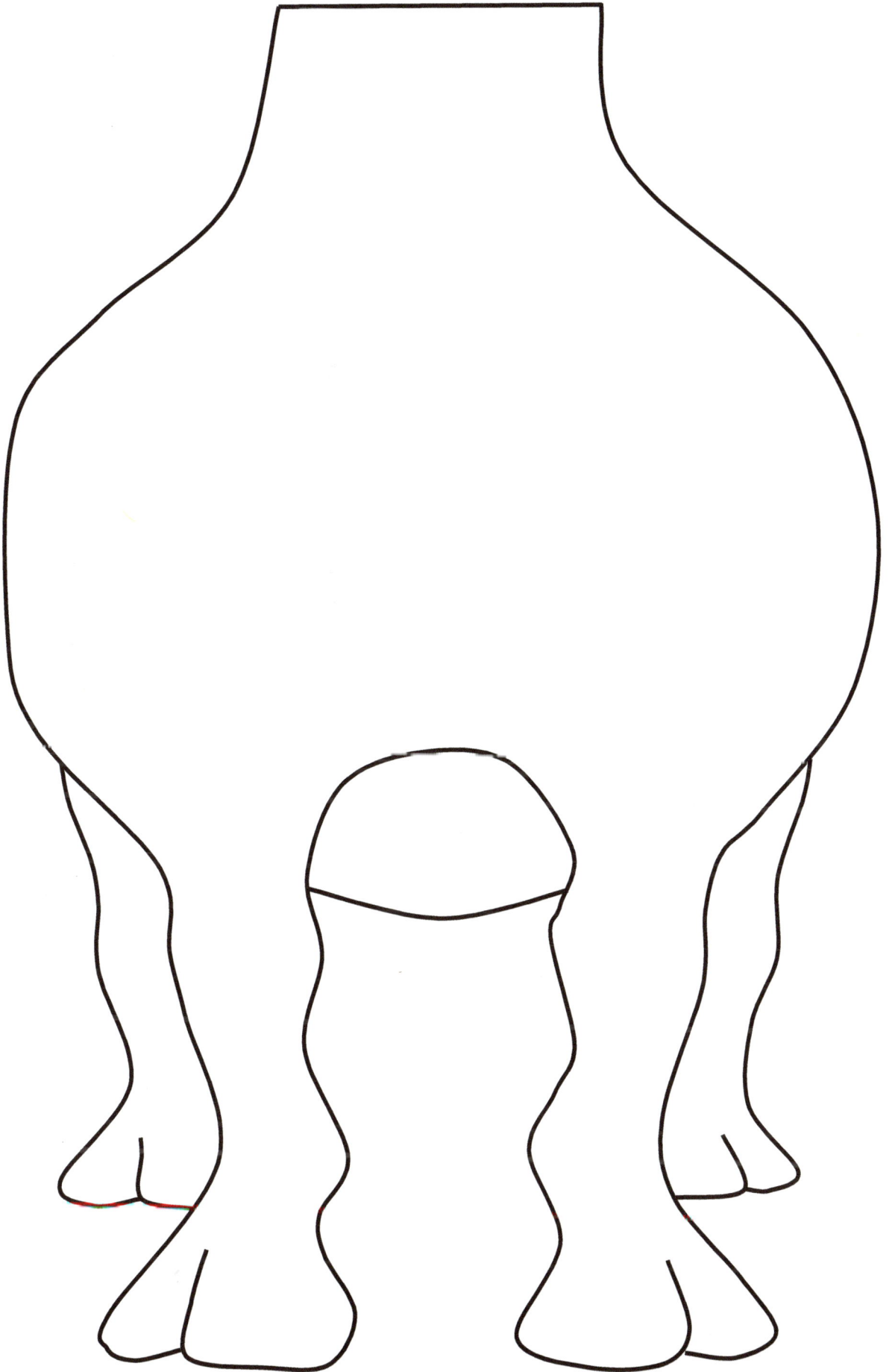

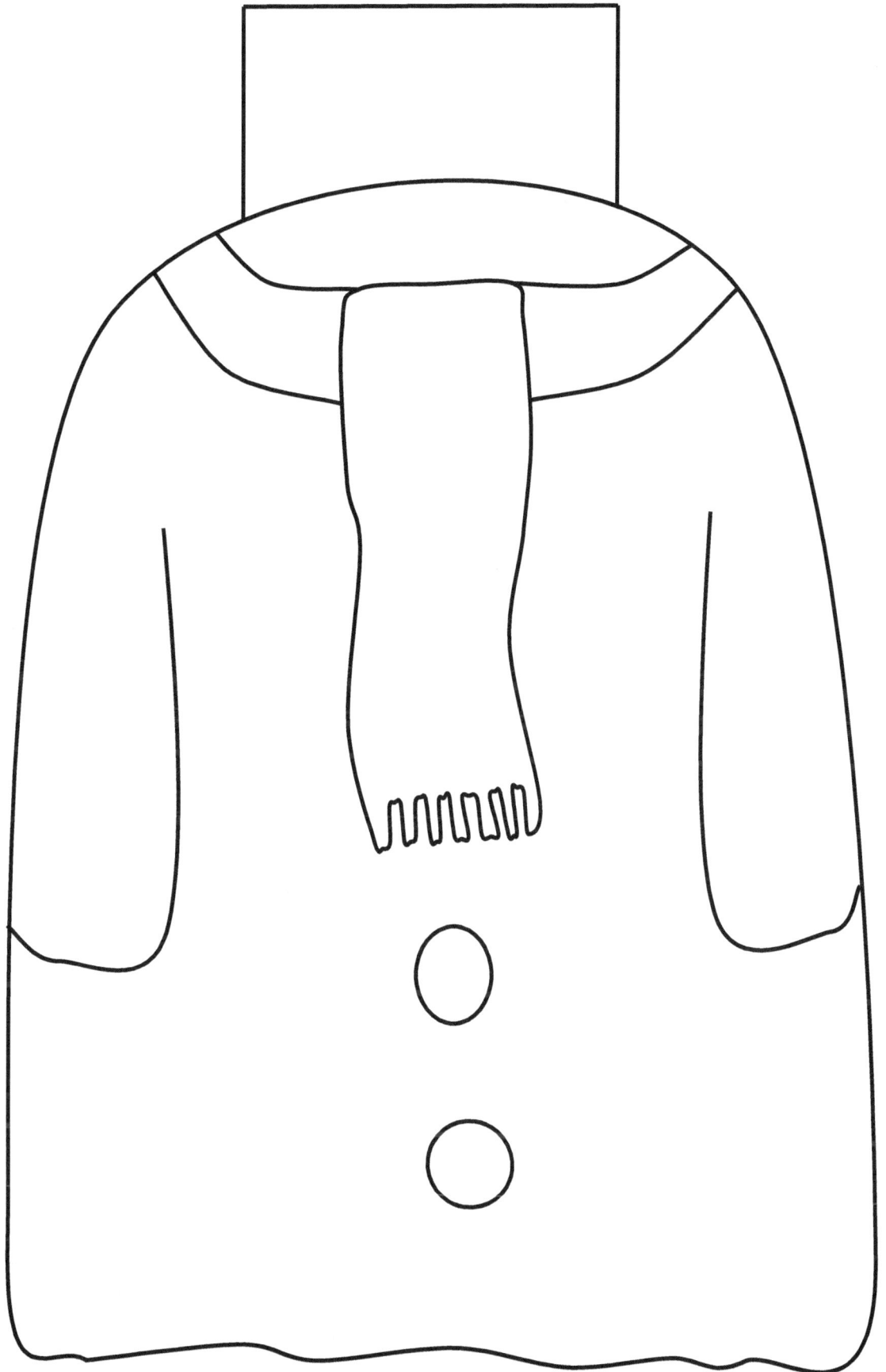

EGYPTIAN PHAROAH (Head)

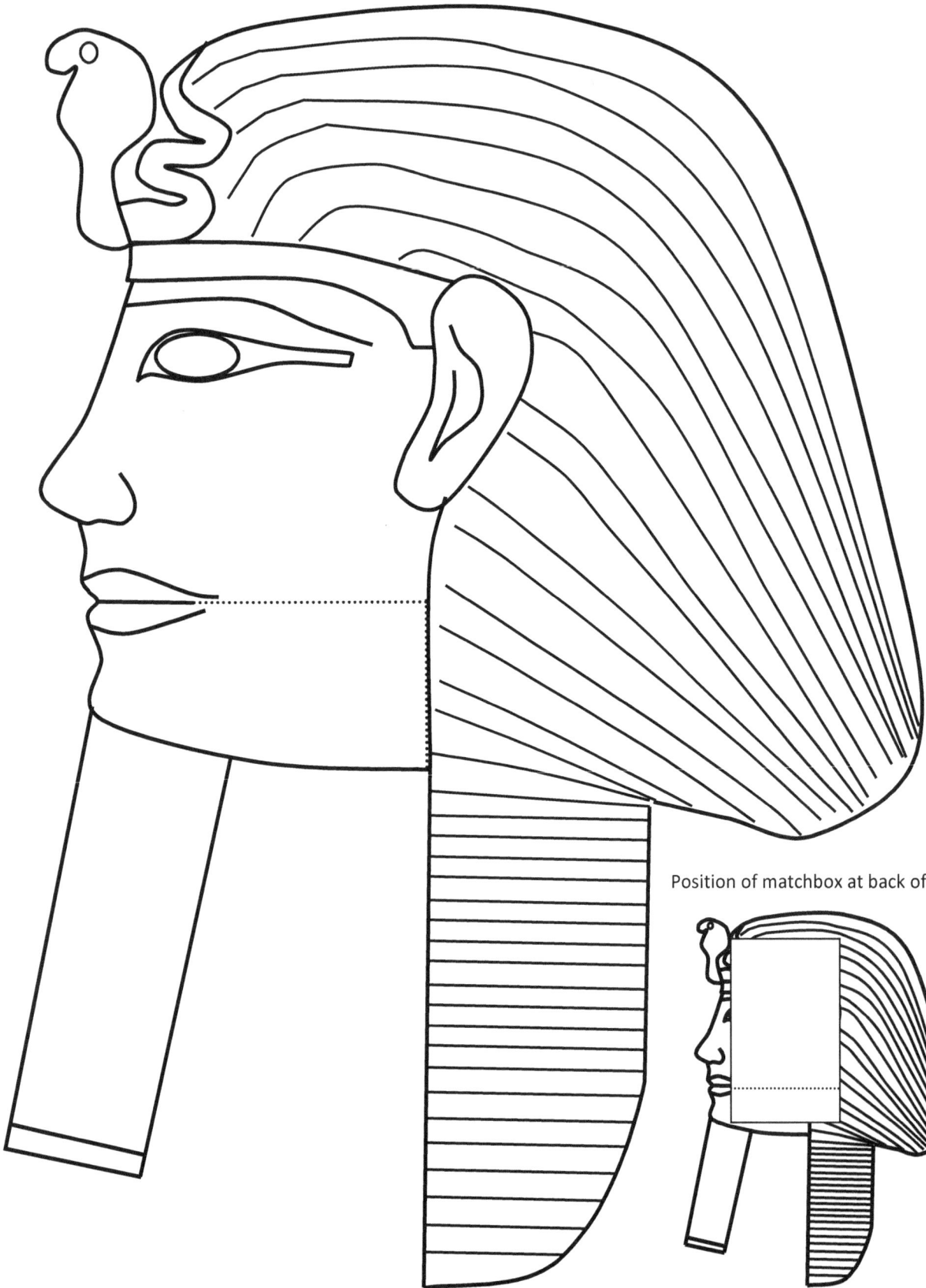

Position of matchbox at back of head

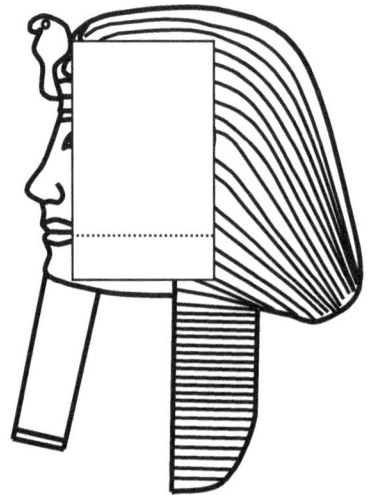

EGYPTIAN WOMAN (Head)

Position of matchbox at back of head

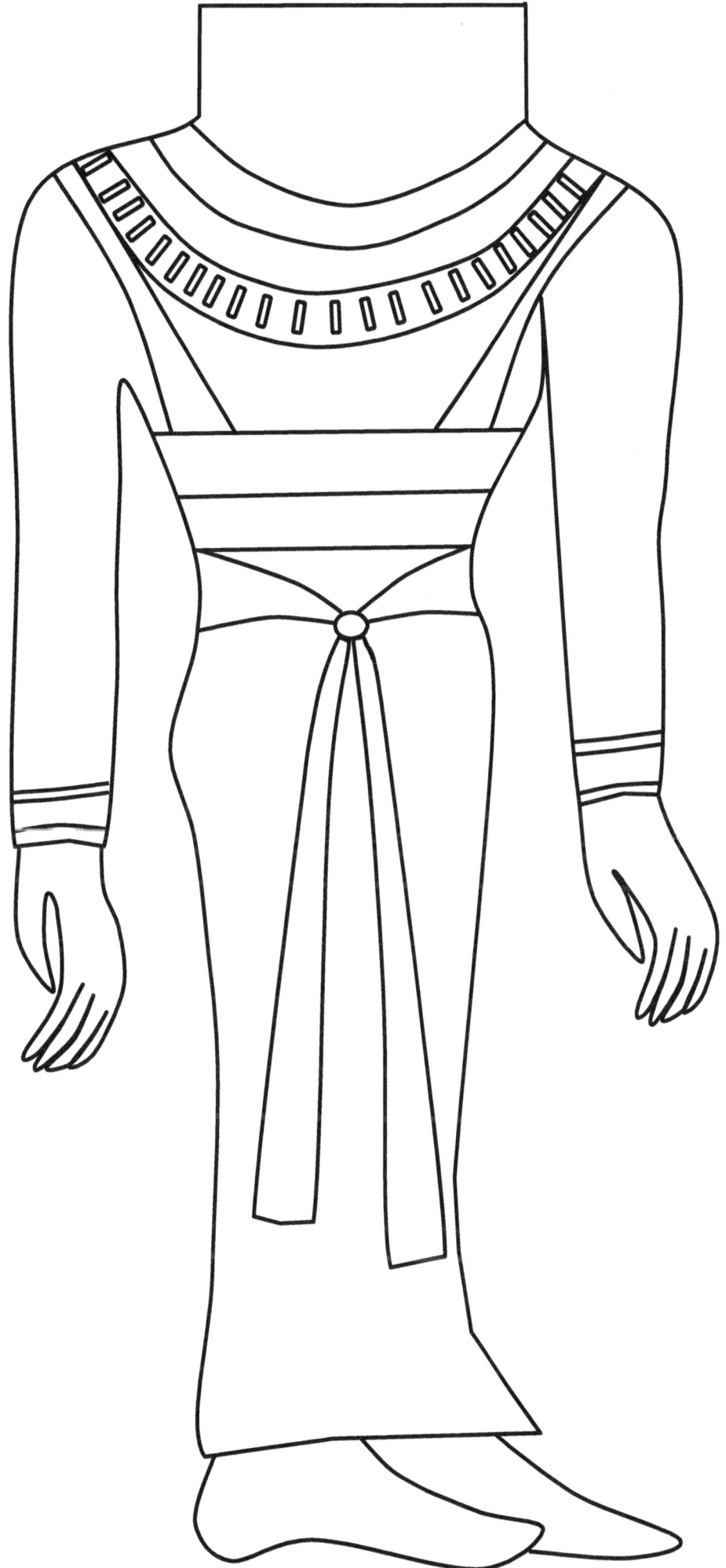

ANCIENT GREEK BOY (Head)

ANCIENT GREEK SOLDIER (Head)

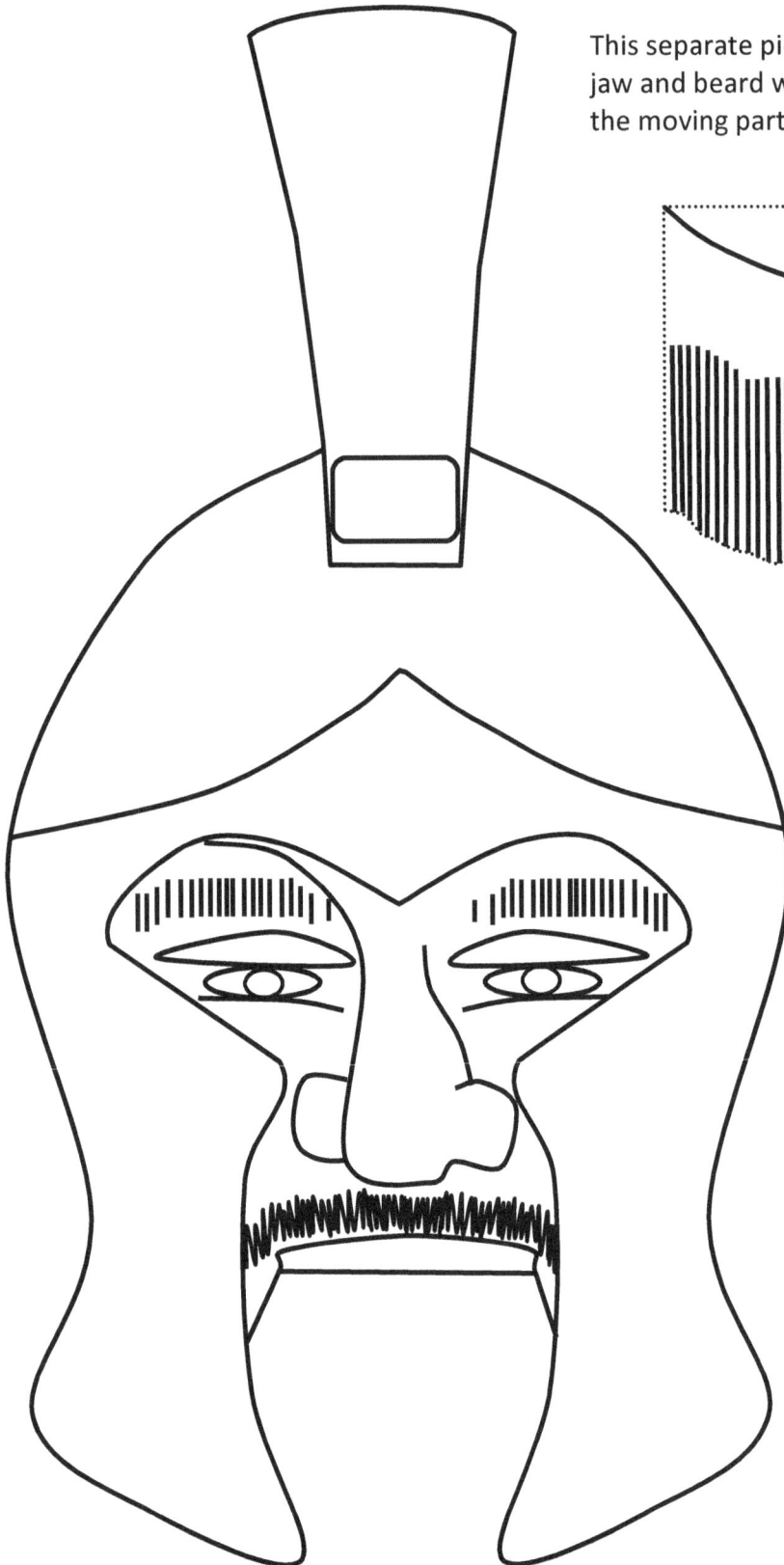

This separate piece is the bottom lip, jaw and beard which should be stuck to the moving part of the Matchbox

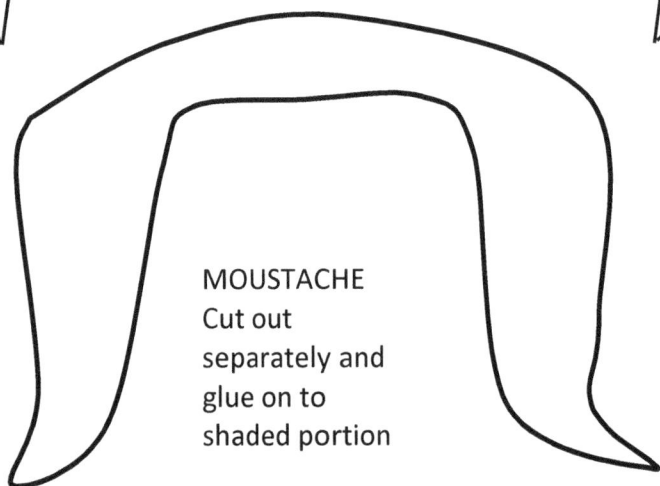

MOUSTACHE
Cut out
separately and
glue on to
shaded portion

VIKING (Head)

This head is slightly different from the others. Cut out the bottom lip along the dotted line. When you stick the face on to the matchbox do not stick lower than the top lip, leave the rest of the head free. Glue the piece below (bottom lip) on to moving tray part. That way the mouth will move within the helmet.

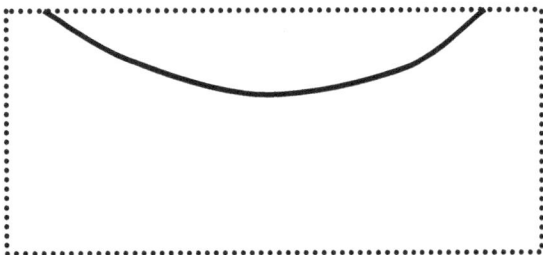

This separate piece is the bottom lip which should be stuck to the moving part of the Matchbox so as to show through the mouth hole in the helmet.

This shows the position of the matchbox glued at the back of the head

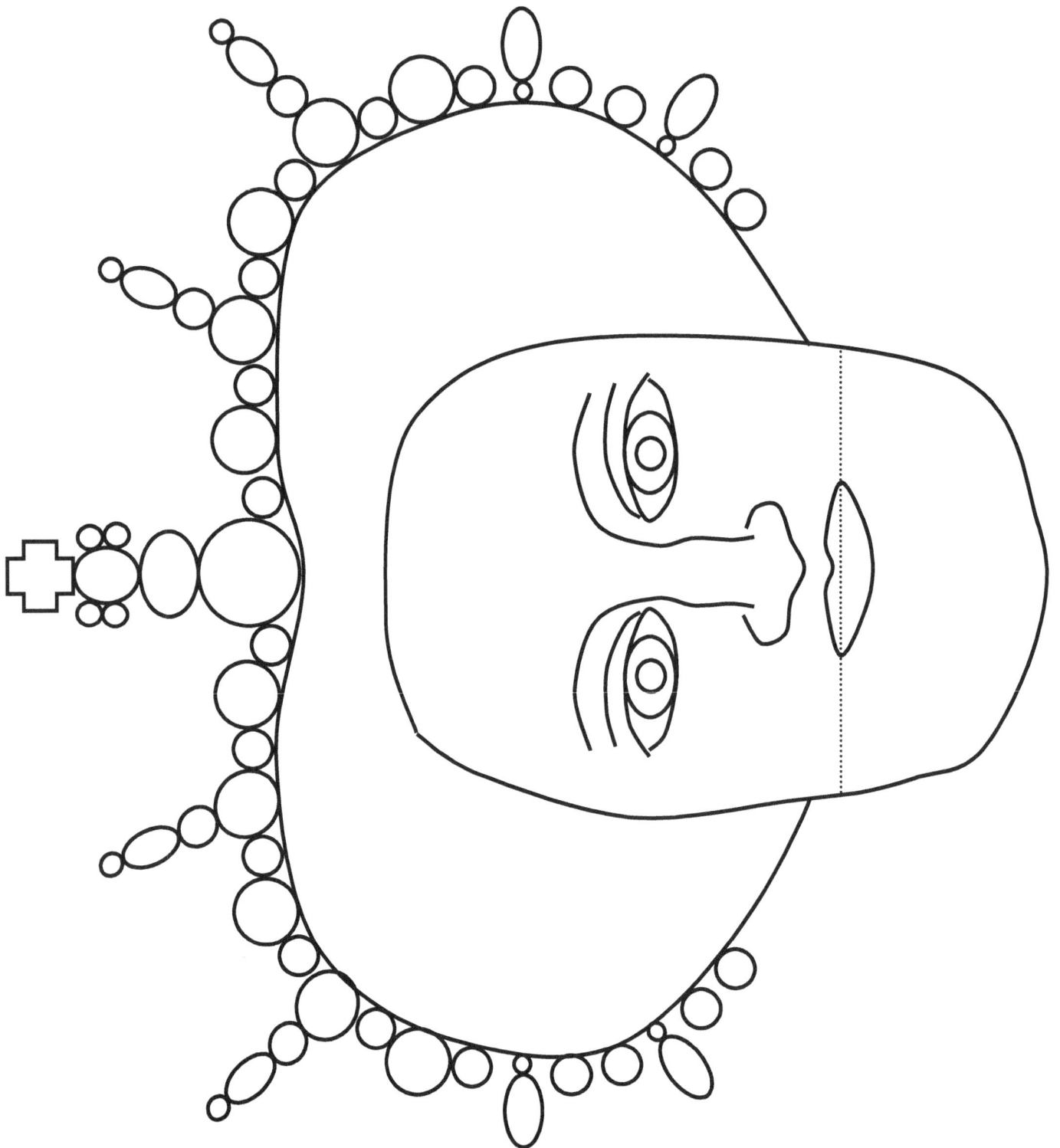

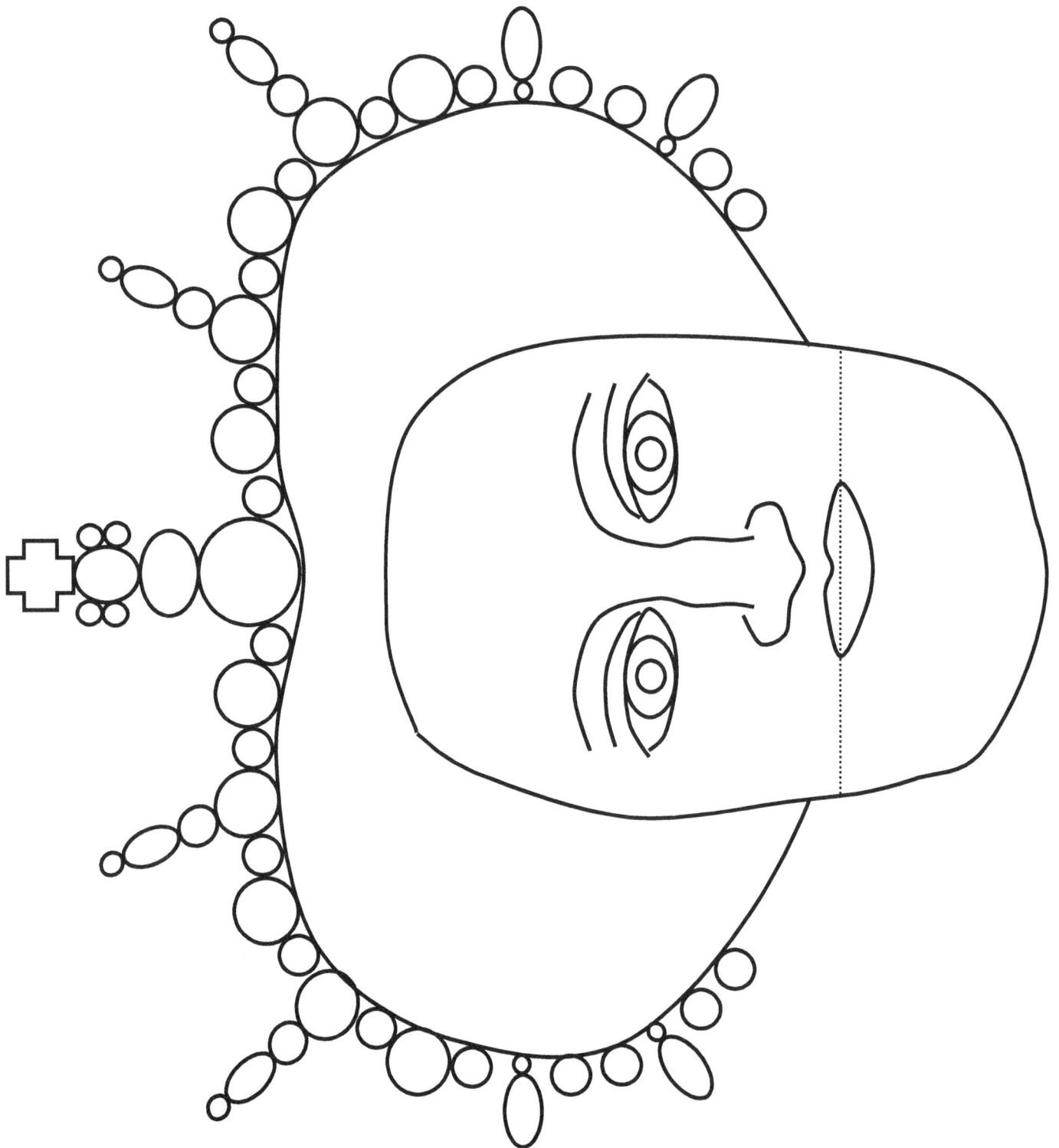

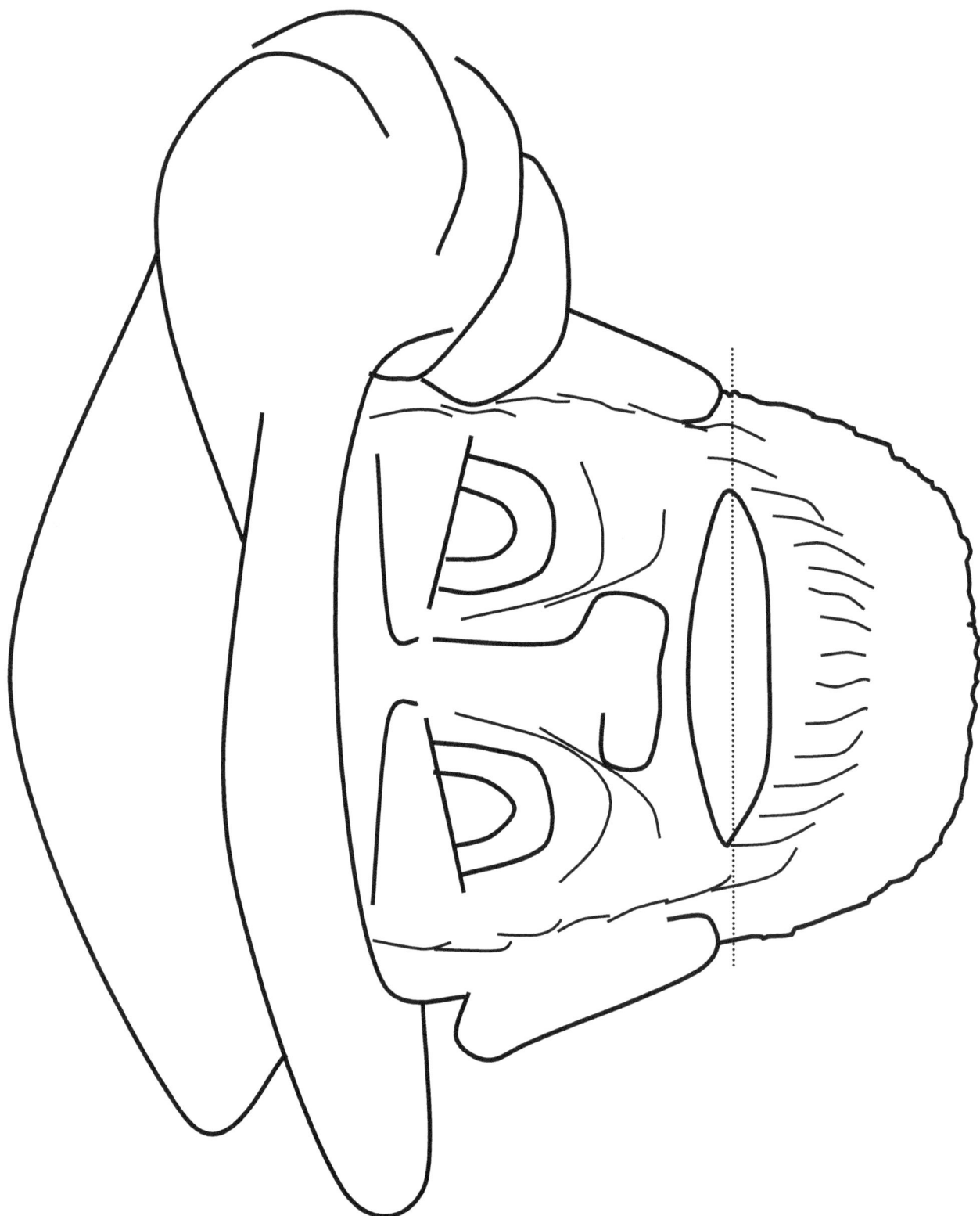

PIRATE (Head)

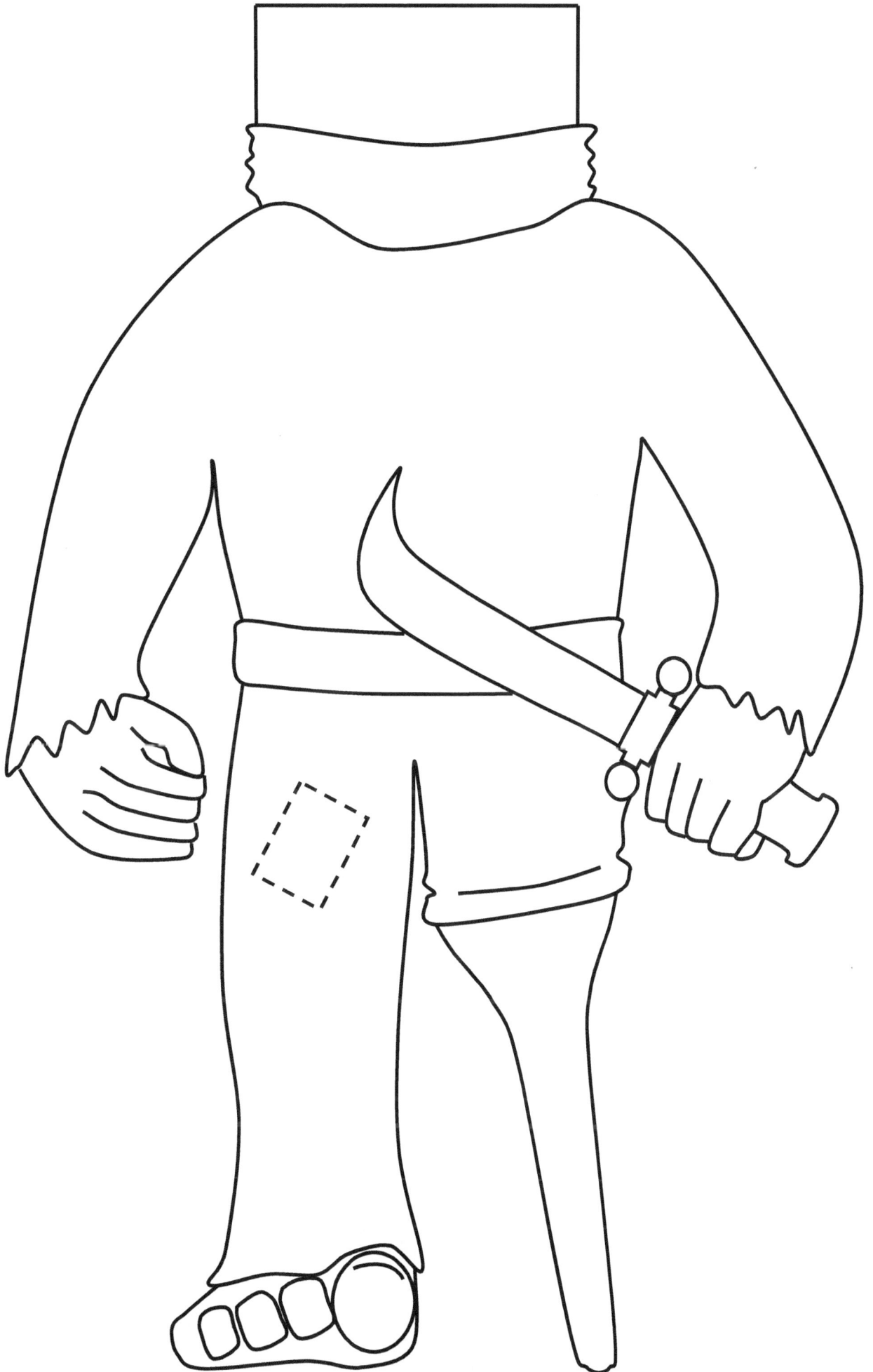

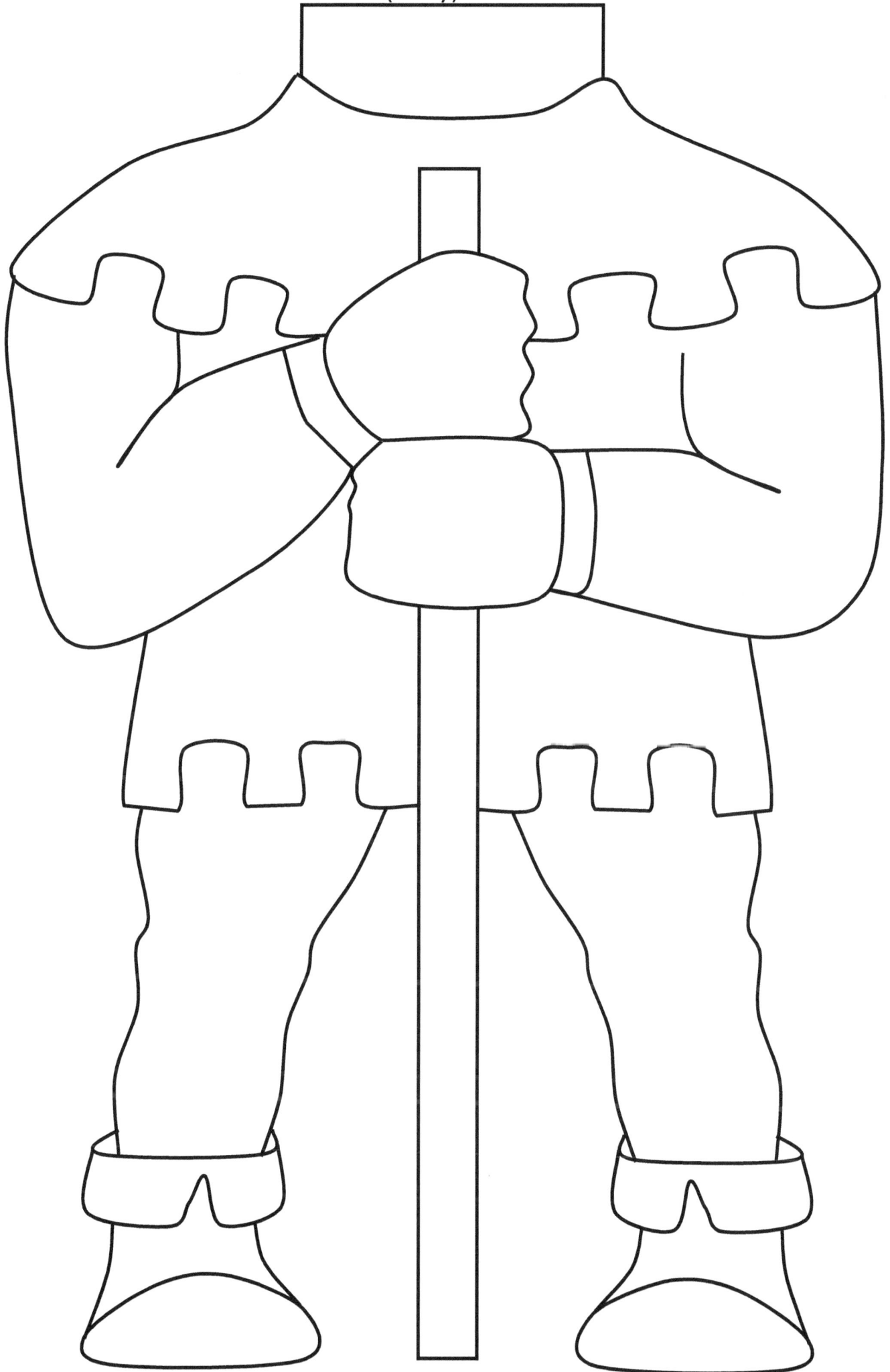

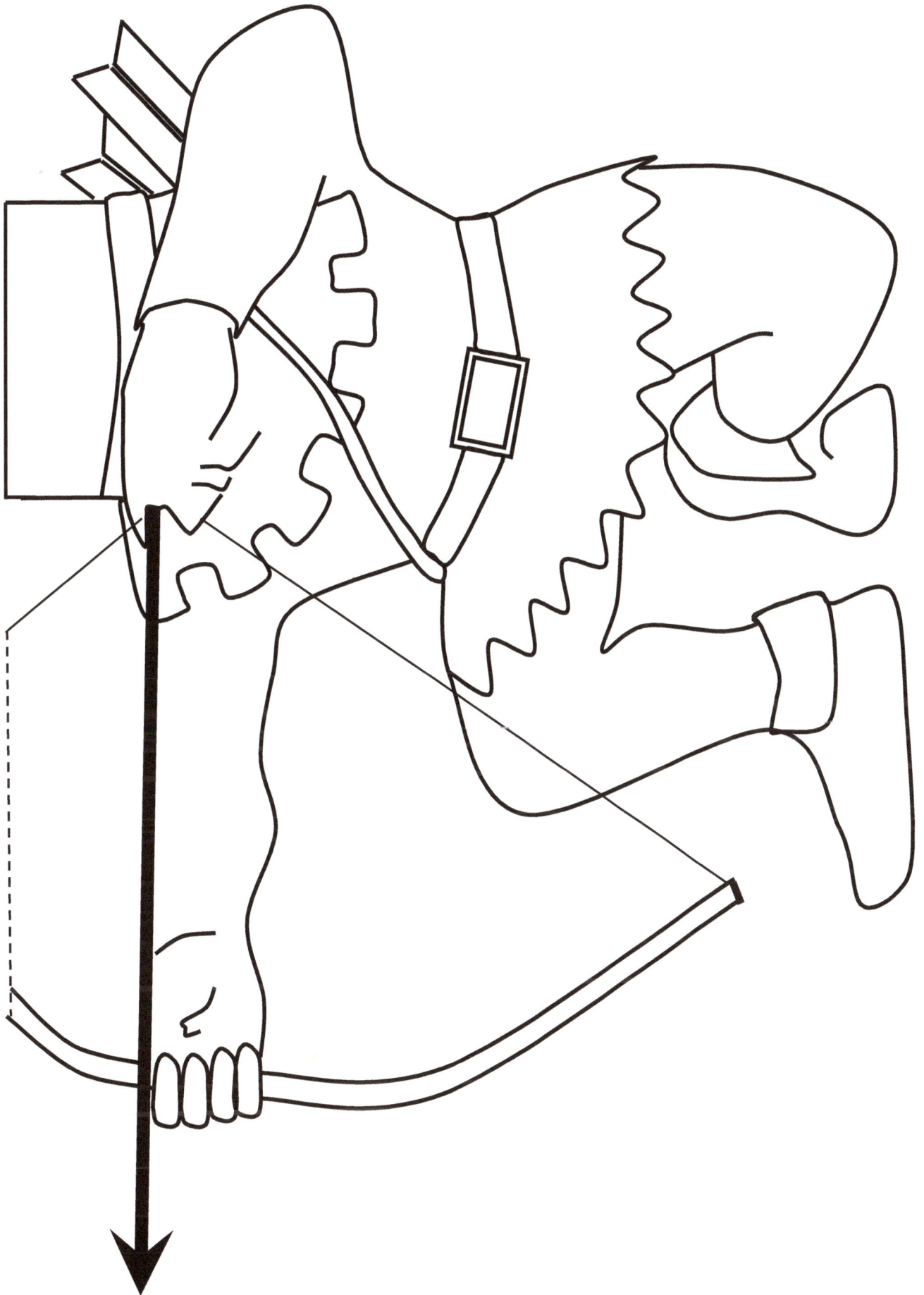

STAN LAUREL (Head)

OLIVER HARDY (Head)

A NOTE REGARDING MATCHBOX SIZES

The heads of the puppets throughout the book are printed at the correct size for use with a household-size matchbox prepared as given at the beginning.

There are only two exceptions: the two dogs (pages 10 and 11) are intended to be used with a matchbox of normal size.

However should a smaller than household-size matchbox be used (eg Swan Vestas, Cooks Long Matches etc) it will be necessary when photocopying to reduce the proportions of the head by adjusting the percentage setting on the copying machine.

To copy for use with a Swan Vestas box the page should be set to copy at 75%.
To copy for use with an ordinary match box the page should be set to copy at 55%.
As copying machines vary this may necessitate some trial and error with the percentages.

The accompanying body, too, will have to be reduced by the same proportions, using the same percentage, although as the body is merely attached by the neck to the back of the matchbox sleeve this is not as critical.

www.ingramcontent.com/pod-product-compliance
Lightning Source LLC
Chambersburg PA
CBHW081543090426
42741CB00013BA/3245